The Pocket Mentor for Video Game UX UI

Want to work in UI/UX in the video games industry? Then this is the book for you. This book provides all the essential information and guidance you need to understand the industry and get your foot on the ladder.

This book provides those both familiar and unfamiliar with the wonderful world of UX and UI in video games with a concise but informative breakdown of the disciplines. It discusses the different career paths and how the role's impact, responsibilities, and perceptions have evolved. This book covers everything, from the education you'll need to searching and applying for jobs, and the interview process. It also includes advice on what to do once you're in the role, with chapters covering best practices for UI/UX, how to set goals for future career progression, and interviews with top tips from experts in the industry.

This book will be of great interest to all aspiring game developers looking to work in UI/UX and beginners looking to grow their careers.

Simon Brewer is Principal UI/UX Designer for Supermassive Games in Guildford, United Kingdom.

The Pocket Mentors for Games Careers Series

The Pocket Mentors for Games Careers provide the essential information and guidance needed to get and keep a job in the modern games industry. They explain in simple, clear language exactly what a beginner needs to know about education requirements, finding job opportunities, applying for roles, and acing studio interviews. Readers will learn how to navigate studio hierarchies, transfer roles and companies, work overseas, and develop their skills.

For more information about this series, please visit: https://www.routledge.com/The-Pocket-Mentors-for-Games-Careers/book-series/PMGC

The Pocket Mentor for Video Game UX UI

Simon Brewer

CRC Press
Taylor & Francis Group
Boca Raton London New York

CRC Press is an imprint of the
Taylor & Francis Group, an **informa** business

Designed cover image: Jenny Brewer (*www.missjenart.com)*

First edition published 2025
by CRC Press
2385 NW Executive Center Drive, Suite 320, Boca Raton FL 33431

and by CRC Press
4 Park Square, Milton Park, Abingdon, Oxon, OX14 4RN

CRC Press is an imprint of Taylor & Francis Group, LLC

ISBN: 9781032433981 (hbk)
ISBN: 9781032433974 (pbk)
ISBN: 9781003367116 (ebk)

DOI: 10.1201/9781003367116

Typeset in Times
by codeMantra

For Zoë, Chorizo, Friends & Family

Contents

Foreword

It is with great pleasure and a profound sense of pride that I introduce you to this remarkable book on UI/UX design mentoring in video games. As a fellow game developer and the founder of Limit Break Mentorship, I have the unique privilege of witnessing firsthand the transformative power of mentorship within the ever-evolving, dynamic realm of the video game industry.

When I first started in the industry, I didn't even know UI/UX was a discipline, let alone a viable career in video games. Being self-taught for most of my professional life, I had to learn by doing and by failing. You can imagine just how much I craved a guiding light, be it in the form of literature such as this book or another dedicated designer with many years and titles under their belt to tell me if what I was doing was right. Consider yourself lucky to be able to hold a book like this in your hands and to learn from those who came before you.

This endeavour represents a convergence of two passions dear to my heart: UI/UX design and the nurturing of aspiring talent. I recognised the crucial role that mentorship plays in the evolution of any creative discipline, particularly within the intricate landscape of video game development. It's not merely about imparting knowledge but about breaking down the barriers of entry and lifting everyone around you. Mentorship is a circular effort—receiving and giving love and effort purely because you want others to do as well as you have.

It fills my heart with joy that, as an industry, we are more than willing to drop the ladder behind us and share this space with new and enthusiastic talent. The pages that follow are a testament to the commitment, dedication, and boundless creativity of the UI/UX designers in this world of game development.

Through the lens of this book, you will embark on a journey that unravels the intricacies of UI/UX design in video games, from the conceptual stage to the final, immersive experience. And I, for one, cannot wait to see what your mark on the industry will look like.

Anisa Sanusi
Founder of Limit Break Mentorship & UI/UX Designer
London, October 2023

About the Author

Simon Brewer started working in the games industry in 2008 at Rebellion, where he discovered his natural skills and deep appreciation for the industry. An avid gamer and a natural investigator, he soon found himself thriving in the User Interface team and has enjoyed many years in various senior roles since.

Simon has worked on several titles for Rebellion, Gree, Rocksteady, Unbroken, Sony, and Supermassive Games and provides freelance work as a self-employed graphic designer. His passion for accessibility and equity in gaming transcends his love of the industry, demonstrated through his many fundraising events, mentorship, and, more recently, his work with BAFTA Young Game Designers.

Outside work, Simon enjoys watching movies, spending time with family and friends, and perfecting his smoked brisket as an amateur pit master.

These days, Simon works as Principal UI/UX Designer for Supermassive Games in Guildford and lives in Surrey with his partner and little dachshund, Chorizo (he's the one on the right).

artstation.com/bunnyballball
linkedin.com/in/simon-brewer-221b5524/

Prologue: Cold Open

Darkness.

Infinite blackness.

Cracks of blinding light slowly creep in, stinging your weary, bloodshot eyes. Everything feels like it's in slow motion. Unfamiliar detritus float past your face. A flashing light in the distance engulfs the metallic void in a hellish red glow. An ear-splitting siren echoes through the hull of the ship. You feel weightless floating in the Zero-G. You sense something has gone horribly wrong.

Reaching out for whatever you can, you drag your floating body slowly forward. Each hand desperately grasping for something to aid the gruelling horizontal climb. With each exasperated breath filling you with overwhelming dread. Suddenly, a charming and catchy show tune begins to play inside your helmet, reminiscent of an old-timey jingle from a radio show or an advert for a children's yoghurt. A friendly green light and thumbs-up icon pops up on the visor's display, followed by a tiny line of scrolling text. Each line follows in sequence, pushing the previous out of sight. It reads that *your oxygen... is running... low...5%... remaining.* With newfound haste and appreciation of life, you summon all your might to pull yourself towards a vast, elaborate console in what you now recognise as the ship's Command Deck.

The console is covered in all manner of different buttons, display screens, lights, flags, labels, cuckoo clocks, dials, whistles, spirit levels, and valves. After what feels like an eternity, you spot a small section in the lower right-hand corner. With a wash of relief, you spot the words EMERGENCY LIFE SUPPORT. You quickly toggle the switch beneath ACTIVATE, and a once-hidden control panel flips into view.

A mysterious LED display presents a text message: DO YOU WISH TO ACTIVATE LIFE SUPPORT? Sequentially followed by two flashing buttons labelled YES and NO. Without thinking and without question, you press YES, revealing yet another physical control panel. Upon this new panel is a big red button, with no discernible indication of its purpose. It appears to be made from felt, the kind of material you would find adorned on a clown's nose. Next to the big red button is an old rusty pull cord, like the one you might find on an old-fashioned lawn mower. Its function is also unclear.

After rotating the last control knob, spinning the random gameshow-style dial, holding down the STOP button for sixteen seconds, and signing up to the mailing list, you confirm that you have read and accepted all the terms and conditions, which, of course, you haven't. In sequence, you bash flashing keys with a mallet as they present themselves to you, dance in time to the prompts displayed on the dazzling floor mat, and honk the bicycle horn as instructed. A cuckoo clock bird eventually pops out noisily from its enclosure, ostensibly signalling a completed procedure.

And then ... silence.

In desperation, you frantically toot the horn a few more times.

Nothing happens.

The alert siren in the background dissipates into a soft hum. Two display bars pop up playfully on the console screen, flash, and then fill towards each other. They spin counterclockwise before collapsing in on themselves and eventually disappearing. A green sad face emoji pops up on the screen, followed by a prominent tick symbol. Realisation creeps in that the oxygen in the helmet has, over time, grown stale and thin. You take one long, withering look at all the widgets and spinning gizmos before you and wonder...

Who the hell designed this?

Mission Control

1

INTRODUCTION

That prologue was a bit dramatic. But by the end of this book, my point about the importance of user interface (UI) and user experience (UX) design will be crystal clear to you. I'm confident that you, as an intelligent reader, will grasp these concepts and their significance. So, let's embark on this journey together, and hopefully, you'll find it as enlightening as I do.

So, what is UX UI? I hear you cry out. Deep down, I feel you already know.

Let's imagine for a moment that you have not heard of it. Many people haven't, but they've seen it and used it. I spend many winter holidays explaining (and re-explaining) my job to friends and relatives.

You might be an industry professional who works with User Interface and User Experience developers and wants to know more about it. Maybe you want to understand the terminology better or utilise UI/UX more effectively. (From now on, I will predominantly use the acronyms UI and UX. Mainly to help me control the word count, and I fear all the repetition will result in me resembling Jack Torrance in the later scenes of *The Shining*.)

You may be a budding video game student, intern, or independent game developer wanting to learn more about the roles and their functions or even start a new career. Regardless of which camp you fall into, there should be something to take away from the bowels of this vast mammoth of a 'pocket' guide.

HISTORY *IS* EXPERIENCE

Before I explain everything about UI and UX in games, let's appreciate how it all started. Full disclosure: what follows will only be a fleeting glance

DOI: 10.1201/9781003367116-1

of history—a crude summary of a great story. It's a subject that transcends video games and technology, expanding into human psychology, cognitive processes, and philosophy—perhaps the subject of my next book (you're right; I should finish this one first.)

Desperate attempts and not-so-subtle hints to the publisher aside, there are some fantastic publications and articles about UI/UX and its history, which I urge you to pursue further. In fact, I encourage you to explore everything I outline in this book in greater detail. Remember, this is a handy guide you can reach for any time. But it's simply that, a guide.

Please don't take my glossing over any people or key events I may miss as a sign of disrespect or an indication that they are unimportant. I want this history to be a concise introduction, but I promise you, I won't go too far back in history…

Since the dawn of humankind, we have explored how we interact with each other, our environment, objects, and technology. The origins of UX can be traced back to Ancient Greece or even 4000 BC China where the importance of *Feng Shui* was recognised. The age of primitive tools saw early humans drawing simple (but consistent) symbols of people, trees, and animals to communicate with each other. This later evolved into symbolic hieroglyphs, became more widespread, and was used for writing, storytelling, and documentation. Technology may have advanced, but we still use iconography (emojis) to express subtle and complex emotions that require no words.

Pioneers in the early 1900s attempted to improve workplace efficiency using the scientific method. Typewriters, looms, and industrial machinery were soon scaled to suit humans as operators, using their hands and feet on the controls. The machines *were* the 'user interface.'

With the invention of the cathode-ray tube, we started to see 'graphics' displayed on screens. The invention of UI evolved with the help of a series of innovators, each improving on their predecessors' work. In the 1950s, an American inventor, Douglas-Engelbart, led the development of the basic graphical user interface (GUI). In the 1970s, the world was introduced to computers designed to support operating systems based on a GUI.

The Psychology of Everyday Things (eventually *The Design of Everyday Things*) was published in 1988 and written by Don Norman, a cognitive psychologist and designer whose book is a must-read and modern-day staple in the design community. He focuses on user-centred design (UCD), meaning design for real people. He considers design with an empathetic eye and less on areas like aesthetics. The book covers many practical aspects of design, including affordances (a property of an object that clarifies its possible uses) and feedback (the reaction or inaction property). He is often credited as the father of UX after joining Apple in the 1990s as their User Experience Architect and coining the term 'user experience design', applying his design philosophies to the software. The term was circumscribed to cover all aspects of someone's experience with a given system.

As you can see from my reckless whizzing through the timeline (aside from making some historians very sick), there is far too much to cover in the time we have.

The first non-commercial "video game," *Tennis for Two*, used an oscilloscope as the interface, with no on-screen scorekeeping (the scores were written down hastily on lab notes). In contrast, in the 1973 game, *Pong* displayed a score on screen. But what else should be considered part of the user interface? The paddles? Is the maze in *Pac-Man* the UI *and* the environment? In a modern game, is everything we see an interface, including the rocks, trees, and laser guns? Interface or not, it's all part of the user's experience. Elements in the gaming world can just as easily convey information and natural affordances as they do in the real world.

A few decades ago, games were not complicated and were made by fewer people than today. The needs of the 'user' were more straightforward. Much of the curated menu, interaction 'experience,' and graphics were mainly created by programmers and (if needed) whichever artist had the spare time. The UX design came passively as a result of *designing a game*. The term itself wasn't strictly used or associated with UI. Designers would make games, test them, and, if it felt right, shipped them.

The UI in games was often a necessary afterthought. No defined roles specialised in it. No one was explicitly paid to pick fonts, draw icons, design interactions or information hierarchies, or curate the flow. I am not saying this work didn't happen; the responsibilities fell onto more generalised and established game development disciplines as tasks. Fast-forward to the emergence of smartphone mobile technology, apps, and dynamic websites, the processes and disciplines associated with UX and UI scaled massively to meet a greater demand for usability. The games industry evolved as more complex systems and technology advanced. Bigger games, higher budgets, and more awareness resulted in a need for specialist individuals to answer the call, as consumers' significant desires for better products escalated the need for studios to up their game. UI/UX could no longer be *just* an obligation.

DEMYSTIFYING UX AND UI

The relationship between the game and the player is a two-way street. The information presented and how the player interacts with that information are ultimately critical in making a game an intuitive, smooth, and painless experience. UX and UI are often seen to be interchangeable, but they are not the same. Some people complain about a game's terrible UI, whilst others praise an excellent experience navigating the same menu. UX or UI can be the saviour or, equally, the downfall of each other.

UI and UX are well-defined in the tech space and critical to product development. UX encompasses *everything*, focusing on the user's first contact with physical and digital products and the whole experience onwards. Meanwhile, UI focuses on visual interaction points (predominantly digital) that permit those interactions to occur. This doesn't mean those working purely in the UI sphere of the UX Venn diagram don't care passionately about the entire experience. They have an invested interest in not being the demise of the other.

However, the design of the game UX differs from what is expected in our streaming services, apps, and websites. Those products specialise in reducing friction so we can order our pizzas and play our favourite shows as efficiently as possible. We don't want to jump over hurdles and flaming pits to get our food delivered, but in games, we do. UX design in games is the careful balance of friction. Of course, this doesn't mean we intentionally design our menus to be annoying. Gameplay presents challenges to the player, and UX is there to help them enjoy overcoming them. That's when games become fun and engaging.

Hunt for the Unicorn

2

ROLES AND OPPORTUNITY

UI/UX is a rapidly growing field, gaining respect as a crucial discipline in gaming. The increasing demand is a testament to its importance, as more studios recognise the need for user-friendly, accessible games. This growth makes UI/UX professionals integral to the industry's success. As costs surge and product choices saturate, a 'good user experience' is no longer a desire but a necessity.

In the game industry, UI/UX roles and responsibilities are rife with contradictions and misinterpretation, with many specific and sometimes overlapping responsibilities.

Researching this area hasn't been easy.

When reading this, people may scream, "That's what I do, but that's not my title," or "Those people don't do that." I will do my best to be as accurate as possible, but it's still a young industry that's constantly changing, and studios don't follow a template. I may skip a few as they ostensibly perform identically under a different name, but people will still swear they're different jobs.

When scrolling through job openings, you might assume you don't meet the qualifications simply because of the role's title. Many sound like a dilution of others. This doesn't negate their legitimacy or utility. It could suggest a studio has the budget to divide the responsibilities amongst multiple specialists or that they need someone to fulfil a targeted need. You may find that some descriptions even contradict each other. And therein lies the point: think of the following as merely a guide.

UX Researcher

This role plans, designs, and conducts research activities with players to help teams understand the target users. They perform qualitative and quantitative research, engaging in empathetic enquiries and user observation to help define the user needs. The research is then used to inform and develop content requirements and design.

Researchers have keen skills in data analysis and synthesising data into clear findings. This allows designers to challenge assumptions and increase consensus among the team with cold, hard facts.

Deliverables include:

- Defining user personas (a fictional character in user-centred design created to represent a user type)
- User stories (an informal description of a feature written from the perspective of the end-user)
- Journey maps (a visual representation of the player's experience)
- Usability reports
- Heuristic evaluations (players don't always want their hand held and must learn)
- Various other research reports that help inform decision-making

Researchers must remain aware of social and technological changes. They perform Inclusive research with all types of users to help teams make accessibility-centric decisions. Researchers will have strategic insight into the studio's objectives (sometimes at odds with what the users want) and will align this with user research processes to formulate objectives that align with the organisation's needs. Thorough research is critical to a project's long-term success. The timing of information is equally important. An essential skill is knowing how to embed iteratively and collaboratively into the workflow to produce timely findings.

You will often see these roles in larger studios, mobile games, and studios specialising in live service games or games as a service. In smaller studios, these responsibilities are often dispersed amongst the development team, or they are carried out by the publisher or the production team. Without the support of a dedicated UX researcher, initial design decisions are often based on assumptions, biased market research, and personal preferences, which can lead to more costly iteration to address user needs.

Interaction Designer

Interacting with something means we influence or incur a reciprocal action. Interaction designers define this interaction by focusing on enabling meaningful communication between players and technology from moment to moment.

Interaction designers will produce low-fidelity wireframes (simple, bare-bone outlines of a digital screen) that communicate interaction solutions and prototypes for later deployment in usability testing. The interaction designer's mission is to ensure every interaction is enjoyable (even amusing) and pain-free. Interaction designer's responsibilities are often absorbed by UI/UX designers or game designers.

UX Writer

UX writers, sometimes referred to as "content designers," "copywriters," or "content strategists," work closely with UX designers to deliver 'copy' (displayed content) to be utilised in the game. Writers help consumers by establishing a solid brand position and clear communication. This includes providing guidance to ensure clarity in interactions. They are responsible for delivering grammatically correct and appropriately formatted text with a tone suitable for the project and organisation's goals.

Many small studios lack dedicated UX writers, so game designers, directors, and scriptwriters often produce copy. This can lead to biased or personalised content that may contain unnecessary detail. Finding the right balance is crucial: it should appeal to the audience but avoid imposing personal agendas. The copy is for the player, not for the writer.

A good writer won't smother the player while still effectively conveying the design intent. They empathise with the user's desires, embody the brand, and work collaboratively with the team. Excellent communication, humility, and immense creative writing chops are essential.

UX Architect

This is a specialised role where UX design and information architecture meet, but it is often absorbed into a UX director or game/design director role. Their primary concern is information structure, ensuring products fulfil users' needs, with content and features organised in an accessible, intuitive, and complementary way.

Their main deliverables include:

- Creating a hierarchy (how all the contents are arranged in order of importance)
- Creating a navigation map (how the user will move through all the contents)

- Conducting user research and interviews
- Testing and translating analytical data (to improve the design from a big-picture perspective)

UX Designer

It would be reductive to say UX designers are generalists. If they're on a team without the other specialist roles mentioned earlier, they usually cover the entire gamut of critical stages of the UX design process.

Their duties include:

- Researching
- Data collection
- Defining user personas and journeys
- Designing navigation
- Conducting user research
- Usability testing
- Producing usability reports
- Feature design and ideation
- Prototyping
- Low and high fidelity wireframing

Some even go further by defining the interface's style and creating assets. However, their focus will primarily be on determining the general experience. An even more significant aspect of the job is getting management, directors, and production *'on side'* or *convincing* them to agree and invest in the production of features to improve the player experience. This can be the job's most complex, painful, demoralising, and rewarding part.

UX/UI Designer

Although they may not technically do every aspect of UX in extensive detail and often have to settle for what they can control, they are a conglomeration of everything: artist, designer, implementor, and researcher. As artistic endeavours and branding fold into one, there is a responsibility to balance form and function.

Their duties include:

- Creating high-fidelity UI concepts
- Pre-visualisation (pre-viz)
- Animation, iconography and typography style

- Visual effects
- UX research
- Interaction design
- User flow documentation
- Depending on the studio, they may also implement UI designs in-engine.

You may see the UX/UI part flip around, implying one outweighs the other. Studios often label the roles differently. **Ultimately, the order isn't important.** Inconsistency in language and conflation of responsibilities are not priority issues in the industry (there are much bigger problems), but they confuse what people can expect from each role. How much UX knowledge is expected of someone who holds this title? Not every company can afford a one-hundred-strong UX/UI team with specialised roles, and we can't always expect game developers to focus on the entire UX process or create stunning UI art.

I've been in this lane for most of my career, and although the titles vary, the responsibilities remain the same. You must perform various activities with one eye on the pipeline, allowing you to grow and learn more or specialise in parts you enjoy.

UI Designer

Typically, a UI designer designs the user interface but doesn't do UX, though undoubtedly, due to the industry-wide inconsistency of it all, they will still dip into many aspects of UX design. They may be artistic or technical, sometimes neither. Often, it's another variation of UX/UI designer and will encompass many of the same responsibilities. It all depends on the studio and the duties they define in the job description.

UI Artist

UI artists might strictly make interface graphics. Some UI/UX teams have dedicated artists who visually realise the designs provided to them. But, much like the UI designer role, the range of responsibilities can be expansive and often not what you would consider an *artist* to do. It depends on the studio and the individual. The title is usually reductive or erroneously used to organise staff through a macro discipline (the art team) that only makes sense to those organising a studio. It may simply be how the studio has always labelled that role, even though the artist is responsible for all the design work. This might be why the art director appears confused when they discuss UX principles.

Visual Designer

Visual designer would be a better way of describing the previous role. They are responsible for defining the style and integrating it with brand identity. They have a keen eye for detail and create beautiful, engaging, immersive, easily consumable, and aesthetically delightful visuals. The role focuses on creating a cohesive and consistent visual language throughout the game, with the interfaces complementing characters and environments to create a more immersive experience for players, making the game feel polished and professional.

UI Technical Artist

This role acts as a bridge between the creative and engineering sides of UI production. The demand for this dedicated hybrid has grown with the rise in more dynamic and ambitious features, technological improvements, and player expectations. I would theorise that it's also in demand as progressively fewer UI artists and designers implement in-engine, focusing more on design and visuals. It's an excellent role to consider specialising in if you are looking for your niche.

The responsibilities can be vast and often dependent on the problems others are trying to solve. If the UI artists wish to create something complex, a technical artist (TA) will consult on the technical constraints and optimal implementation. They make helpful tools to improve the team's workflow and take on more challenging feature requests.

Other responsibilities include:

- Optimising assets
- Identifying technical issues and solutions
- Liaison between art and engineering departments

Essentially, they manage the reality of what's achievable while helping open the door to what's imaginable. They possess contemporary knowledge of UI art techniques and development processes and can adapt and innovate using new technologies. Proficiency in code, mathematics, scripting, and art generation skills is essential in balancing fidelity and performance.

UI VFX Artist

Usually, the visual effects (VFX) team provides ad-hoc support for UI features. The UI technical artist may take on these tasks. A dedicated UI VFX artist is a luxury often found in large-scale studios. These specialists make FX for in-game communication in the world space, like the arc you see to show you how far your grenade will go or the area the player shouldn't stand in when something is about to explode. They will also create effects to provide feedback for gameplay events, like unlocking new items/skills, loot box reveals, and fantastical, celebratory moments, like when a character 'levels up.'

They possess a robust knowledge of node-based shaders, particle systems, textures, and geometry manipulation. However, due to the nature of the UI discipline, they require a slightly different mindset. They must be far more user-focused than FX-driven to communicate feedback clearly to the player.

UI Scripter/Implementer

In some studios, the UI artists and designers may never touch the engine. As part of the workflow pipeline, they will be focused purely on creation and design. Their job is to take finished designs into the engine. This could be due to a lack of available skill sets, a bespoke engine, or the speed of production that requires that type of workflow.

They focus on layout, data structure, and logic, working closely with artists and designers to implement features based on the delivered designs. Like the UI technical artist, they act as a bridge to the programming team. Once a design or concept is approved, it is handed to an implementer who breaks down the assets, optimises them, builds the structure, and hooks it into the engine.

UI Programmer/Engineer

These developers are dedicated to UI engineering and breathe life into UI. They flip the switch and manically scream, *"It's alive, it's ALIVE!"* They possess a solid understanding of game design principles and programming languages. UI programmers collaborate with the team to balance design, artistic goals, and technical requirements for performance. They form the bridge between the backend and the presentation layer.

One of their primary responsibilities is ensuring an interface is responsive and smooth. They optimise the logic and code to provide exceptional performance on multiple platforms. The role requires them to consider technological constraints and prioritise project needs while facilitating innovation and artistic endeavours. The UI programmer plays an essential role in the video games industry, and, frankly, we'd be screwed without them.

UX Strategist

The UX strategist focuses on the overall UX vision and, you guessed it, strategy. They consider the "big picture" and how to achieve it. The role sits between manager and director, as a liaison between business and player. They consider the business's goals and how they can create value through innovation while reducing costs. They validate the user research to ensure it meets objectives and often help establish team composition. A thorough UX strategy allows executives to understand UX value and helps the team stay on target.

The manager identifies issues and opportunities through competitive analysis, ensuring end-user needs and preferences are considered. Leadership, communication, and business acumen are taken into account.

UI/UX Manager/Director/Head

This role provides leadership, direction, and structure. A crucial part of the role is collaboration with their team, other directors and leads from the Art, Design, Programming, and Executive teams. They are responsible for directing, coaching, and mentoring a growing team of varied UX/UI skill sets and establishing the studio's UX/UI culture. They help improve processes to achieve excellence across multiple projects and ensure that user experience is intuitive, engaging, and enjoyable for the player through empowering their team.

They are at the helm, driving the direction and meeting company and product goals. This requires:

- Thorough understanding of the user
- Strong artistic and design vision
- Clear directives and articulation of strategy
- Organisation
- Open communication
- Guidance
- Empathy

They often provide concepts, style guides, and supporting documentation to provide clear visual direction and maintain high-level consistency. Managers also frequently work with external developers and suppliers to offset the internal team's workload when it reaches capacity.

The definition of a bad director is someone who tells everyone what to do and how to do it. A good director requires humility and empathy. They're there to encourage, coach, clarify goals, and be proud of the results. Managers are responsible for nurturing their teams, helping them grow and achieve their goals.

Unicorns

In the context of a working environment, you would rightly assume that a 'unicorn' alludes to some one-of-a-kind, mythical anomaly—a rare creature to be revered and looked upon in astonishment and admiration. The term 'unicorn' refers to an individual with unique skills and attributes that cover the expanse of an entire discipline, sometimes called the "full stack." Variations include "half stack," where an individual is proficient in all areas of the technical side or in all areas of art and design. Unicorns are highly adaptive problem solvers known for their creativity, innovation, and out-of-the-box thinking. Although these traits are highly sought after and encouraged in anyone, no one actively tries to recruit a 'unicorn.' You won't find that term used in a job advert.

I've yet to come across someone who describes themselves as one. I've met many great individuals who certainly fit the bill, though. These individuals typically grow within an organisation and have experienced numerous product life cycles. They've achieved a holistic balance between working and learning, and their wealth of knowledge helps others grow.

In short, the majestic unicorn is a valuable asset to any team or organisation and is highly prized for their unique talents and abilities. Fingers crossed, you'll encounter one in the wild.

UI or UX?

Roles and responsibilities within UI/UX teams vary widely across studios and organisations. The titles associated with these roles will not always accurately reflect the actual duties and expectations. A UI designer typically collaborates closely with a UX designer but, due to industry-wide inconsistencies, may often delve into aspects of UX design, too. Similarly, a UI artist might initially focus on creating interface graphics but find their responsibilities expansive and not necessarily limited to artistic work. Other specialised roles in a studio, such as game designers, 2D artists/illustrators, technical artists, and VFX artists, may all contribute to the user interface and experience. The variation in titles and responsibilities demonstrates the need for a broad understanding of UI/UX pipelines and the capacity to adapt within these roles.

Regardless of title, all suitable candidates share these common traits:

- Communicate clearly and fluently
- Always prioritise user experience over user interface
- Keep the player as the primary focus
- Employ brevity, consistency, and familiarity

- Be aware of common traits, trends, and functions
- Prioritise accessibility
- View data analytics as a driving force rather than an obstacle

Some people in the industry misinterpret their duties. At times, I've found the overlap, dilution, and consolidation of roles frustrating, and it's been challenging to articulate the differences accurately. There is a lot of "gatekeeping" on social media platforms. You see discourse from "tech-bros" screaming, *"That isn't true UX,"* and constantly arguing about it. It's so boring because it doesn't matter. There's so much jargon that it becomes unbearable, overinflated, and self-important.

Ultimately, the players don't care. Yes, UX designers do a lot. No, UI and UX are not the same. Yawn.

Finding your Unicorn

Striving to be an expert from the start is ambitious but unrealistic. Is it better to be a generalist or a specialist? The industry needs both, and it will serve you well to be both. A specialist does well at digging deep into the details, whereas a generalist can see the bigger picture and broaden our understanding. At the start of your career, you need to strike a balance. It will be valuable to generalise your responsibilities, learn as much as possible, and specialise more later.

When I started, only a few of the aforementioned roles existed. I came from a background where you had to do everything. I've often wondered how enormous studios with armies of UX and UI developers navigate the environment without stepping on each other's toes while remaining invested in the outcome despite so many layers of separation. Regardless of whichever role you choose, you'll undoubtedly spend a lot of time explaining what you do and convincing others to let you do the job you were hired for.

SENIORITY

Seniority in the workplace refers to higher experience, expertise, and responsibility. It can imply a longer organisational tenure, more decision-making authority, and leadership responsibilities. Seniority can influence factors such as pay scales, benefits, and opportunities for career advancement.

In my experience, a more accurate indication of someone's true seniority is their relationship with feedback. How well one gives and reacts to feedback indicates professional maturity, and one's title might not reflect this. I've seen directors slam their fists on the table until they get what they want. I've witnessed companies promote the wrong people for the wrong reasons, and I've observed rookies with a breadth of knowledge some might take a whole career to procure. You can see and experience true seniority in how people act, listen, and learn.

However, claiming it is not enough, and people need to see it demonstrated. You must be comfortable critiquing yourself in the open for others to witness. Many leaders are uncomfortable doing this, as it may be seen as a weakness. Being able to articulate your weaknesses and areas for improvement demonstrates strength, providing a catalyst for people around you to employ honesty because you show that you can handle it. Arguing with constructive feedback is pointless. It's an opportunity to show *how* you can improve yourself by being *willing* to improve.

To increase your chances of getting promoted and becoming better at work, avoid the following behaviours:

- Expecting a promotion without demonstrating value
- Engaging in gossip, lying, being untrustworthy
- Acting entitled rather than being proactive
- Failing to advocate for yourself
- Not being a positive team player.

The Intern

An internship is a short professional engagement, typically lasting a few months. These positions are primarily available to students, but budding developers can often apply. Attaining these positions is fiercely competitive, as the pool of candidates is vast. It's an opportunity to gain professional experience—something most future employers demand but, paradoxically, is hard to acquire. At the end of a successful internship, there is the potential to be offered a permanent position, but not all studios do this. Some won't offer work experience initiatives due to concerns over leaks, legal issues, mature content, capacity, cost, or infrastructure.

A bad studio will make an Intern do the 'grunt work' that no one else wants to do. There's a good chance they won't coach, educate, or even pay you. However, a good studio will hopefully pay you (it won't be a lot) and treat you as if you were an associate or junior—and a human. For them, this is a genuine initiative for the future, not free labour. You'll be treated with care and given meaningful, achievable, low-risk work. You'll be assigned a senior developer to be your new coach, who will show you the ropes and give you meaningful tasks to help build your confidence, experience, and professional soft skills. These first jobs are essential for building foundational skills, making connections, and kick-starting your career.

The Junior/Associate

I prefer the term associate to junior as it sounds less patronising. Some studios use both terms. I've also seen it referred to as assistant, and *you don't want to know how I feel about that one.* Their responsibilities and tasks should be educational and achievable, and problems should not result in discouragement or negatively impact the product. These tasks are more isolated and allow juniors to learn new things and make mistakes while removing the negative implications if challenges arise.

We need more junior developers! You'll hear plenty of developers screaming this. It's a major issue in the industry. To add insult to injury, since 2022, there has been a surge in redundancies. Even after significant efforts from many studios to create junior positions, the heartbreaking fallout is that many are now out of work. The job pool is now saturated with experienced developers competing for the few remaining positions alongside recent graduates.

Meanwhile, slashed budgets and headcount further impact the games industry's hunger for more complex products with shorter deadlines. Some studios focus purely on hiring highly skilled seniors only, as they have more experience, deliver faster, and carry more responsibility—but they're expensive. Juniors and associates are cheaper to hire but require more overhead to train and supervise, which takes away productivity from the seniors assigned to them. It's a brutal juxtaposition. Equally, just *finding* seniors has become difficult, as they are reluctant to give up permanent roles in this climate. The irony is that juniors *eventually become seniors*, and if this trend doesn't improve, we will see a future where there's no new yield.

Through coaching and encouragement, juniors will learn the ropes, discovering how to pace themselves and pick their battles. Seniors share their experiences and knowledge, demonstrating how to adapt when new technologies fail—things you only learn 'in the field' when you *gotta do things the old-fashioned way, kid.* Moreover, seniors will be challenged by new minds and new perspectives. The fantastic benefit of having a mix of seniority levels in a team or studio—especially junior roles—is how it creates culture. Juniors bring new ideas and are greater advocates for social and cultural changes that promote more inclusive and accessible ideologies. They are not afraid to speak their minds and share their views. Great ideas come from anywhere, not just from the top.

Mid-level

Post-junior, a developer with two to four years of experience or at least one production cycle completed will progress to a mid-level position. Having built confidence and skill, they will be entrusted with more feature ownership. Compared to juniors, they require less supervision and quality checks but still benefit from regular mentorship and coaching.

Senior

Once a developer has demonstrated that they are self-sufficient and capable, they will be promoted to senior. With more years of experience working on various titles, they can fully own features, coordinate with management and teams, and require little supervision. Seniors will support the leadership team by mentoring junior, mid-level, and intern developers.

Studios often introduce intermediary seniority levels using a ranking system or adding prefixes to the seniority level to offer "more" promotions. For example, they use expert or advanced to describe a junior or senior with more responsibilities or skills. I often see people who consider title as their only metric for career progression, so if they aren't getting regular promotions, they feel unfulfilled and slowly become disgruntled. Stagnation can arrive when the ceiling for promotions declines. Or they leave and go somewhere else to climb the ladder. I can only assume this is an initiative employers instigate to reduce the number of people bashing down the director's doors or planning some overly complicated *'looks like an accident'* scheme to acquire the top role.

As you progress in your career and gain seniority, your path will depend on your personal and professional goals. You might be happy just earning money, doing your job making cool games, going home, and enjoying your life pursuits—and that's totally fine. You'll be seen as the rock by your team, the reliable backbone, and the master of your craft. If you have interests outside your current path, assessing what you genuinely enjoy and where you want to go next is essential. You could shift your focus towards people and project management or perhaps direct art and technology. Alternatively, you may become an expert specialist in your chosen field.

Lead and Principal

Discipline leads can take several forms. Some focus on people management, logistics, scheduling, and the team's welfare, while others can be purely technical. Depending on how big a studio is and how many projects it has on the go, there might be a lead per project. Part of the role is coordinating your team's schedules and collaborating with production to devise a comprehensive plan. All leads represent the discipline and must advocate for its interests.

The people manager encompasses more than just approving annual leave; they guide, nurture, and offer compassionate support when needed. Remember, your team members are not *'underlings'* or *'subordinates,'* as I've heard managers say in the past, but rather your peers and fellow humans. Your primary focus should be serving them, establishing benchmarks, helping them envision their goals, and leading with a positive example.

Not everyone is cut out for leadership and people management, and that's fine. Sometimes, individuals get promoted to a leadership position simply because they excel in the skills of the discipline, but that doesn't guarantee they will be good leaders or people managers. An expert at a craft doesn't necessarily equate to a great people manager. This sort of promotion often results in the team losing one of its best producers since leads don't typically contribute to the team's tangible output. If you feel that leadership isn't your calling, you can choose to specialise further and become an expert in your craft, like a principal.

Though both are ultimately recognised as experts in their field, the primary distinction between principals and leads is that one focuses on the team, while the other focuses on excelling the discipline's practical capabilities. Principals can absorb all the features and run independently, becoming valuable sources of knowledge and support. Leads and seniors can look up to them when they need guidance or face extreme technical challenges. Juniors and other team members might see them as inspirational (I did). These individuals constantly research and master new practices and technologies, and their expertise raises the bar for the team's combined output.

Directors

In most cases, the 'end-game' is the director (or head) position (or, I suppose, starting your own studio). Directors must often let go of their practical involvement to focus more on direction, logistics, and management. In this position, you'll manage the artistic and design direction, advancement of technology and pipeline development, outsourcing management, and human resources. The responsibilities of this role are similar to those of a lead but have greater accountability regarding the project, the team, and how you represent the department amongst the other directors and studio.

Basic Training

3

SHOW VS TELL

For a chapter focused on education, this will undoubtedly sound very stupid. As a kid, I had no idea how video games were made. My brother and I would create games on the BBC Micro or with the *Doom Engine*, but I didn't think about where the official games came from and who made them. They were just fun and appeared from some magical place. When I started to understand, a career in the industry didn't seem possible. The thought of studying it in further education never crossed my mind. The very idea didn't seem real.

Fast-forward to the present day, and the popularity of the gaming culture is phenomenal. Games have become an enormous business. Ninety-three percent of children in the UK play video games[1]. Unsurprisingly, there's an increased interest among today's students in pursuing games as a career. They have a more comprehensive range of choices and greater access to higher education and commercial courses. The ability to create and even sell your own games at any age, with any amount of experience, budget, or knowledge, has never been more accessible. Easier access to state-of-the-art tools and online resources has significantly lowered the barriers to entry. However, this increasing fascination now includes the challenge of finding the right education path and future employment opportunities.

Attending a specific educational institution or taking a prestigious online course does not guarantee a job. Possessing a diploma does not reflect your employability compared to someone who doesn't. Acquiring the right skills and education to make you desirable to an employer in a fiercely competitive industry can be a truly daunting experience.

It's been a hard time for the industry lately. Since 2022 and 2024, many game developers have been made redundant. So when there are available roles, the pool of candidates is extensive, and it doesn't matter what diplomas

DOI: 10.1201/9781003367116-3

you may have, it's the value you can demonstrate. I'm not saying that higher education and private sector diplomas don't provide value, but the quality of how and what you can *show* as a result of that diploma truly sets candidates apart. What special skills do you have? Do you demonstrate desirable values, character, reliability, and teachability?

In 2007, I left university with a bachelor's degree in music industry management and studio production. I wanted my band to hit the big time, but as a backup, working as a record company scout or music producer would suffice. During the first academic year, my band broke up.

Nevertheless, the skills I learnt to help promote the band such as graphic design, video editing, and website publishing proved beneficial in acquiring much-needed funds. They helped purchase the necessities for an aimless, disillusioned student drifting through a course for which they have buyer's remorse – food, alcohol, and, most importantly, video games. I would sell my services to promoters and other bands around the area and, in the process, unknowingly improve my rough, self-taught fundamental skills—all this while comfortably enjoying exploring the city of San Andreas in the latest *GTA* game.

Regardless of my newfound scheme, I still felt lost. When my course ended, I had no desire or connection with the music industry. I feared going home with no 'next big step.' I had no ideas and felt like a failure. It's an overwhelming prospect for anyone graduating.

Fortunately, hope was not lost. My brother worked at a local independent game studio. I never thought I'd be able to do something like that, as I assumed he had special training, and I didn't. He knew I was competent and had a boatload of youthful energy, so he passed on my CV. It was the only favour I would get. Knowing someone working at a studio is a great advantage, but it's never guaranteed. Vouching for someone can only carry so much weight, and I would only be hired on merit and merit alone.

I applied for a QA role, and the decision was based on my interview and the skills and competencies I could demonstrate. My newly acquired bachelor's degree would only prove so much. Its only value now was indicating that I could show up and finish something—and not much else.

I showed examples of my websites, coursework, and personal and freelance projects that were somewhat relevant. I spoke passionately about games and my work ethic. The interview was followed by a performance test (finding and reporting bugs in the game) and assessing how well I reported them. All I had was my degree, a passion for video games, and this opportunity. It was all on me, and only I could convince them. Only I could screw this up.

Thankfully, I didn't. I was lucky. I cherish every day I get to work in games. I appreciate the people who helped me throughout my career and try to repay it by giving back. A diploma, certificate, or recommendation can only get you so far. Nothing is guaranteed. An employer will primarily assess your character, what you can do, and how you demonstrate it. How do you stand out from the rest of those vying for the job?

GET SMORT

In the past, careers required a qualification even to be noticed, and this is still the case in some industries today. Formal education can be beneficial, provide valuable skills, and help you identify your path, but a degree is not a strict requirement to get a job in the game industry. That said, certification is required for certain positions, and not having one can put you at a disadvantage. A great portfolio and raw talent can be formidable but can only get you so far.

There are pros and cons to the various avenues you can take to become educated and gain experience. Do you crave structure or want complete control? Formal education can be expensive; can you pay a significant fee or incur long-term debt? Just remember, there is no correct way. Every path is different; it just depends on you.

University Degree

After finishing school, students are often encouraged to advance to higher education. This is in addition to equally noble pursuits such as apprenticeships, trades, or entering the working world immediately.

Rewind a couple of decades, and you would be hard-pressed to find many university courses specifically tailored for game development. Most graduates entering the industry in the 1990s and 2000s would have computer science, mathematics, physics, art, or graphic design degrees. Nowadays, there are courses specifically focused on games due to their increasing popularity.

What is worrying is how practical some of these courses are. With so many places offering a game course, how do you know you are getting a good deal and reliable information? Are the credentials and experience of those teaching and the validity of the syllabus being taught relevant? Tech moves quickly, and advancements and processes have accelerated over the past few decades. So, how does one stay up-to-date when providing education?

Having never taken a game course, I spoke with Andy Bossom, Industry Engagement Lead at the *School of Games and Creative Technology*, part of the *University of Creative Arts*. Andrew is also the director of the *UCA Games Incubator Studio*.

> *Games degree courses ideally have a range of permanent and sessional staff with either previous or ongoing relevant industry experience. Within the teaching teams, they'll also have theory and research lecturers, PhD students and professors who are specialists in their related fields, contributing to the subject's forward momentum. Universities with engaged staff and industry-facing research activities will be connected to the industry through collaborative projects, live briefs co-authored with industry partners (like Kwalee, SEGA Two Point, Supermassive Games at UCA), as well as regular Knowledge Exchange activities, or Knowledge Transfer Partnerships. Institutions can utilise national or international research grants to expand their technological offer (to students and in commercial activity to industry), building greater links between higher education and the games industry.*

Higher education can be a financially costly and time-consuming proposition. (Unless you have scholarships or financial aid.) You'll spend many years paying off student debt. This can add tremendous weight to the decision and more reason to research a course that will give you bang for your buck.

> *Higher education in the UK does come with a price tag. With this in mind, it's worth investigating a range of degree courses prior to going to university. Make sure you understand the course, its units and its structure. It's essential to attend open days (both near and far), making sure you speak to both the lecturing staff and students from the course. Look at the range and quality of work coming from the institution. Ask what their alums are doing and who they're working for. Elicit a range of success stories. What competitions, local and international, have their students won or been shortlisted for?*

Paying more doesn't necessarily equate to getting better quality, either. In the UK, for a fraction of the price of a university course, you can opt for a private course and pay a one-time fee. A relatively inexpensive private course run by an industry professional might be well-researched and beneficial. However, the certification might not be recognised. Certifications awarded by expensive courses may be recognised by the industry, but they don't provide the one-to-one mentoring you seek. Some university courses offer cutting-edge technology and have professional industry affiliations, while others include a course in the brochure to attract more students.

> *There's a time cost and greater personal investment that comes with a university education versus a short course. Many benefits are acquired from this additional time spent at an institution, which you would not otherwise have access to at home. Some key positives: regular weekly engagement*

with experienced lecturers who have industry experience, visiting lecturers and live industry briefs, taking part in internal or external game jams with your peers, games industry facing exhibitions and festivals, the opportunity to travel on study trips local and abroad, access to a significantly wider range of contemporary and more expensive technologies related to your subject area.

Many studios will consider your skills instead of your education. However, you may need a degree to work in another country. Each country will have different rules, and you must carefully research your obligations. You'll need a special visa to work in the USA, and strict regulations exist. Generally, to qualify, you need to meet at least three major requirements:

- You need to have a bachelor's degree or higher in a relevant field (also check that the degree counts as a STEM degree, as some less technical courses don't)
- You have to be working in an occupation that's considered a speciality occupation
- You need to have a prospective employer (sponsor) already to arrange for this on your behalf

The structured environment of a university yields many advantages and disadvantages. You have to consider time, cost, and quality. Before one enters a professional workplace, beyond the apparent software and game development skills, studying with peers will help promote soft skills, such as teamwork, accountability, and working to meet deadlines.

I enjoyed my time at university. Even though my course wasn't related to games, it was still helpful. I learnt a lot in and out of the classroom. I made great friends, had interesting experiences, and gained independence. In hindsight, I wish I had done a course more relevant to what I do now. I don't know if they had a games course back then, but they do now. and by an interesting twist of fate, I was recently asked to join my university's Industrial Advisory Board, alongside other alums to help advise on their games courses—an opportunity to give back which I would not have received without the higher education route.

Independent Courses

You may want to avoid student debt, train quickly, or maybe the university lifestyle wouldn't suit you. Parallel to the many higher education establishments, there are equally as many private courses now available in games education. They can be a more affordable alternative to a traditional degree.

A short-term UX design certification program provides a foundation for someone with no relevant experience in UX to become "job-ready." There are eight-week crash courses in website development, graphic design, and game art. These could be suitable alternatives to research.

You'll pay a flat fee to attend in-person or remote classes for a fixed time. Some courses take a few months with one or two weekly classes, while others can be a short crash course, appealing to those who need results quickly. Some don't require you to complete it as you've paid anyway. Many require you to provide your own hardware and software capable of handling the coursework. This, in itself, can be an expensive upfront investment. In the end, you often receive a certificate. Like university courses, the one-on-one element with tutors is part of the appeal. You can ask experts questions directly. The other significant benefit is that you often learn as part of your schedule. Online courses often provide students with access to pre-recorded video lectures and virtual materials, which makes them more accessible for different time zones and lifestyles. However, this can be a disadvantage, as they may not be able to communicate effectively with the class tutor or have one-on-one interaction. Equally, they emphasise individual learning and focus less on group projects, which can reduce the development of professional soft skills.

I stress that some independent courses may not provide the recognised industry value and legitimate certification your future employer may seek. You should verify the course's accreditation and institutional approval, research the provider's reputation, analyse course details and transparency, and look for professional endorsements, student testimonials, and industry relevance. Examine the level of interaction, support, and depth that align with your career goals to ensure you aren't being sold magic beans.

Self-directed Education

Self-directed education may be the right option if finances are tight or you prefer to learn things your way. Right now, you have free access to leading game engines that industry developers use daily. In addition, there are many smaller and simpler engines available. I've worked with BAFTA's Young Game Designers (YGD) and seen many talented kids design and produce fantastic games using free and accessible software. Many industry-standard tools and applications now have free alternatives, meaning you can learn the essential skills without paying for expensive subscriptions.

With these tools and resources available, delving into the world of game development is more accessible than ever. Engines have more intuitive interfaces; there's more documentation, design forums, and a wealth of tutorials online that can allow beginners to grasp the fundamentals quickly.

(Developers working in the industry today still rush to YouTube and forums to learn new things or get help when they are stuck.)

Online communities can create a positive learning atmosphere that allows people to seek collaboration and assistance with individuals with similar interests. This ignites enthusiasm and promotes a sense of empowerment among learners, allowing them to experiment, refine their skills, and bring their imaginative ideas to fruition. You can also contact professionals and industry mentors on social media if they are available. With all these excellent resources, you only need to be dedicated, disciplined, and focused.

Therein lies the downside. Unlike higher education or a course, no formal structure exists for self-discipline. There is a risk of learning inefficient, incorrect, or outdated practices. Your ability to develop soft skills may not advance as much. However, you could compensate by starting small projects with friends or attending game jams (a collaborative game design event) that may make up for this.

It will be up to you to manage your time effectively and create your syllabus. You have to fight the urge to skip the "boring" fundamentals and dive straight into the advanced topics, as this can lead to struggles and could possibly cause you to give up. Yes, you should have fun and enjoy what you do. You should make mistakes and try out new ideas. However, neglecting essential knowledge and having a clear plan could haunt you later in your career, affect your design process, and dent your motivation.

The main challenge is that self-education is the hardest to 'show,' albeit it can be one of the more impressive options when you do. "School of life" doesn't always award the reassurance and confidence some interviewers seek. However, an employer could look at an awarded certificate and realise that someone has completed something, but it doesn't necessarily indicate that they can perform the skill. Practical skills can often exceed credentials. It's critical to show clearly in your portfolio all that you have learnt in extensive detail—even if it was at home on your own.

Internships

During a course, you may be offered the opportunity to go to a work placement or internship at a game studio. You can also apply for this externally if an option is available. Work experience at any stage of your career development will be beneficial regardless of the duration. During an internship, you can gain valuable hands-on experience in the industry and network with professionals, increasing your chances of receiving excellent references after graduation or even a job. Internships are extremely competitive, on par with the *Hunger Games*.

Soft Skills

Transferable soft skills (professional skills) include communication, leadership, time management, delegation, and collaboration. Obtaining these basic professional skills from your education route is critical to being a successful and effective developer. In an organised environment like a university, you will naturally grow your communication skills. You will talk to your professors, lecturers, administrators, industry professionals, and guest speakers. You'll work in teams with your peers and learn the art of collaboration, compromise, accountability, pitching, and teamwork. There are deadlines for assignments, and a schedule for classes and lectures. This aligns with developing a game with milestones, schedules, and a shipping date to hit. While learning at home is possible, it requires organisation, discipline, and commitment to mirror this approach. When doing an online course or self-directed learning, the requirement to talk to anyone is often purely optional.

Networking is critical. Regardless of your education route, accessing a vast network of alums, industry professionals, talent recruiters, and peers is possible at an event, online, or at your place of study. Yes, it can be daunting to approach someone. For some, this may be more of a challenge. If you struggle to find people you're comfortable with, many organisations and communities can help. For example, organisations like Limited Break (www. limitbreak.co.uk) are among the most extensive mentorship programmes for underrepresented people in the UK games industry.

DO YOUR HOMEWORK

I can't stress how critical it is to research thoroughly when considering all your education options. You might be confident about your career goals, or you may not be. You might want to take a more general approach and explore your interests before committing. A degree or certification is a tremendous accomplishment, but investing time and money is not for everyone and isn't always necessary. What I do believe is that you always have to continue building upon your skills.

Location can also be very important, both in terms of overall cost, maybe living at home, versus the lifestyle you would like to effectively study and succeed in your chosen area of study. What would work for you? Do you want to be based in a buzzing city, by the seaside, studying in a quieter part of the country, or with an institution that is part of a creative echo system connected to a nationally recognised and respected games industry hub? What are the priorities, negotiables or must haves? There is a lot to consider before applying for a university education.

My first mentor, a great art director, once said, *"Try to learn something new every day, no matter how insignificant it might appear."* Learning outside the classroom is crucial for gaining a competitive edge. Set aside time for additional creative objectives, learn new software, and participate in collaborative projects to build soft skills. The aim is not to encourage an unhealthy work-life balance. Work hard, but take breaks, keep playing games, and start with small, achievable projects. Every day is a school day.

There are plenty of excellent universities, online courses, and boot camps out there. I know some great developers who run them. There are outstanding and prestigious game-focused university and college courses with excellent reputations that have been churning out alums for decades. But I've never taken any of them, so I can't attest to their quality or recommend any responsibly. Everyone's education experience is different. That's for you to research, and I implore you again to do it. Find a path that works best for you. If you invest time, money, and energy into something, make sure it's worth it.

The best education you can do for free is to pay attention to all the UX and UI around you. It's everywhere.

NOTE

---

1 childrenscommissioner.gov.uk/resource/gaming-the-system

UX
Know Thy User

4

UX IN A NUTSHELL

UI refers to the visuals—the aesthetically pleasing and user-friendly digital elements the players interact with, encompassing everything from layout and colour schemes to typography and icons. UX, conversely, addresses functionality, user emotions, and the reasons behind the existence of those aesthetically pleasing elements. It's concerned with how users experience the game holistically.

UX is about reducing friction to make a particular task easier for the user. However, in games, UX is also about adding friction and removing it to meet the game design intent. UX designers strive to understand who the player is, the psychological aspects of user behaviour, needs and motivations. Only then can they create designs that focus on satisfaction, providing the feel and usability to support the function, ensuring a positive experience from start to finish.

SO WHY BOTHER?

UX can be critical to a product's success or failure. However, some games lack the most incredible user experience or interface and are not highly accessible, yet they still perform and sell well. So why go through all this trouble if some games can get away without offering a great experience?

It could be that the game is part of an established franchise and will sell anyway due to its legion of fans, mass commercial appeal, and dominant

DOI: 10.1201/9781003367116-4

marketing. Or it features fun, engaging gameplay that allows players to overlook the shortcomings of the outward experience to get at the juicy content. Take some lower-budget independent games, for example. They may not have access to vast hordes of UX developers and make do with what they have, but the game is inherently solid and has grown a cult following. Only after the massive overnight success of *Among Us* did the developers quickly add more usability features demand response to audience feedback and access to more significant resources[1].

Players should not need to look for a great experience. They should feel it intuitively and subconsciously.

Useful

If a product isn't useful, then why make it? What is considered "useful"?

Something might not have a "useful" function, but it still delivers an aesthetic or entertaining appeal. Is a painting or a TV show *useful*? Can a game be considered *useful* if the player never accomplishes anything tangible? The high score isn't going to pay your bills, but they can be useful in other ways, such as entertainment, socialising, artistic endeavours, education, therapy, or keeping a child occupied during a long trip. So when does a game become *useless*? A useless game offers nothing. They are switched off, refunded, or uninstalled almost immediately. They fail to provide enjoyment. They are broken, unplayable, or fail to meet the expectations that were set.

Usable

Usability refers to the extent to which a product or system can effectively, efficiently, and satisfactorily achieve specified goals. In other words, it is about ensuring that a product or system is easy to use and that users can achieve their goals smoothly and efficiently. Players get bored and frustrated quickly if a game isn't fun or engaging.

Discoverable

Discoverability means anything the player wants to do should be easy to locate. If something is difficult to find, it is less likely to be interacted with. This heavily influences layout design and the creation of effective information architecture. When you buy something from the in-game store, the designers ensure that the price, your available currency, and the checkout button are easy to find.

Credible

Credibility in game design is a cornerstone that fosters trust and confidence in players. It ensures they feel confident in their interactions and believe their time and money are well spent. This is particularly crucial in a competitive gaming market, where players seek value for their investment.

Desirable

Like it or not, video games are luxury goods. You can't eat them. They won't nourish you, although you can try. Designers communicate desirability through branding, image, identity, aesthetics, and cost. Desirability can affect usability, and while a better-looking product may appear to work better, this isn't always the case. The more desirable a product is, the higher the chances that a player will recommend it to friends or write reviews, and influencers will generate a desire in others to acquire it. Desire also triggers social cues. When we own something desirable and that others want, it can inflate our sense of self-worth and perceived status amongst our peers. This is how the industry can charge a small fortune for cosmetic add-ons in popular multiplayer games.

Accessible

Despite recent strides, game accessibility is often overlooked and neglected. It's not yet the norm, and accessible features are often sidelined or cut. Designing for accessibility is often seen as costly by some, but I believe it's essential. Some features are easy to implement, while others are more complex. When accessibility features are not planned and implemented early, the cost and effort increase significantly. It's important to remember that people with disabilities and those who need accessible features make up a significant portion of the audience.

In UX, designers must research and analyse their design decisions while considering accessibility. They should carefully design features and have plans for players to circumvent inaccessible walls where necessary.

It's not about making games *easier* or *babying* the player. It's not about removing the challenges that make games fun. It's about inclusion. It's about equity. It's about letting players experience the game vision you are presenting whilst providing an escape from the challenges in their own lives that they cannot control. A great designer never neglects accessibility in UX.

Valuable

Value refers to how much a product or system benefits the user. It effectively meets user needs and goals, offering tangible and intangible benefits such as saving time, making tasks more manageable, providing unique features, and ensuring a positive experience. Ultimately, a valuable product or system is one that users find beneficial and satisfying to use.

IT'S *NOT* ABOUT *YOU*

I once worked with a design director who started every discussion with *"I like…"*

Strangely, when you start making a product, you are not making it for yourself. It's not about you. The players are the people who will *use* your product, game, or service. Their needs are the challenges, desires, and objectives. It's okay to have preferences and a vision—otherwise, all games would be the same—but these should concern style, tone, and story.

Players still need an experience they can find usable. It must function, or it fails to be of purpose, resulting in attempts to search for a solution elsewhere. We must employ empathy: what do they need? What do they want? How can we influence them to make choices that align with the journey we're taking them on? UX is not just a singular action. It's not *how* the UI you see on the screen works. We design the entire journey and how we frame the whole ecosystem. *You* have nothing to do with it.

You can make better toast with a hot skillet than with a toaster. It's funny that people are only realising now that the number dial on a toaster isn't about *doneness* but time—and that's why the results are inconsistent. The internal design of a toaster has never really changed. Electricity passes through wires, slowly heating to generate infrared radiation for a specific duration. Sure, there are new features, styles, and improvements, but the core functionality is generally the same. The real question is, why do people want the machine instead of using a hot pan?

Steve Jobs once said, *"People don't know what they want until you show it to them"*—a divisive yet accurate statement. Henry Ford said, *"If I had asked people what they wanted, they would have said faster horses."* People's ideas typically reside within the realm of current knowledge, not in the future possibilities.

If you don't properly understand the user, how can something be adopted and become current knowledge?

Empathy plays a crucial role in design decisions. The *"I like games this way"* approach when making decisions affecting millions of potential players is not empathetic. We are making it for another human. You cannot be Veruca Salt about it with *"I want this, I want that."* Take the time to think about someone else and remove the ego. What works for you might not work for everyone.

UX PSYCHOLOGY

A human being is essentially a brain wrapped in a meat puppet. There is psychology in design. We can't understand how to make something until we have understood people. When users engage with your product, they:

1. Refine the **information**
2. Seek **meaning**
3. Take action within the **time** allowed
4. Store information and experiences as **memories** and **lessons**

A law in design is not a rule imposed by force by some governing body. We're not talking about stealing a car here. It's more akin to science, where statements based on repeated experiments or observations predict a range of natural phenomena. A principle is a fundamental truth, serving as a foundation for a universally recognised belief, behaviour, or reasoning. Design equates to problem-solving, where some rules can be broken, twisted, and ignored. We don't need to reinvent the wheel, but sometimes we want to improve it because the people using it have changed.

Be it law, principle, theory, or bias, we conform to their practice as the majority are based on human behaviour when processing information and finding patterns. Without knowing it, you already practice most of these daily—not just when designing. I've not covered them all, and for the ones I have briefly covered, there is a plethora of information online about them, so I urge you to dig deeper into them. Many of these will make you say, *"I didn't realise that had a name; it just sounds like common sense."* And you'd be right.

Information

Cognitive Bias

Cognitive biases are scientific concepts relating to how we tend to make systematic errors or deviations in behaviour, judgement, or decision-making based on prejudices, social or moral reasons, and our failures in processing information. In simpler terms, our preconceptions influence our choices, leading us to overlook or even dismiss information that contradicts our beliefs, even when that information could be beneficial.

Confirmation Bias

People seek and interpret information in a way that aligns with their beliefs or expectations. This biased approach to decision-making is subconscious and can occur in games when developers make assumptions about what users want without testing with real people. This can lead to software that's unsuitable or unfavourable for players.

Hick's Law

The more choices a person is given, the longer it will take them to decide. Limiting options can reduce decision fatigue. So, instead of presenting the player with a long list of character customisation options, we can stagger it into stages or limit the number to a few critical choices. This can enhance engagement and focus, helping to prevent feelings of overwhelm and frustration. Additionally, if you have more options than are humanly fathomable, provide functions for players to choose favourite items, dynamically sort menus, search, or indicate new items.

Fitts's Law

The time required to move to a target area is based on the target's distance and size. In simpler terms, the closer and bigger a button is on a screen, the easier it is to click it and reduce the risk of errors or frustration. How you pad your interactive elements (adding negative space between elements) can be improved by applying this law. This can enhance gameplay and immersion. For example, when the jungle explorer must perform a quick time event

(QTE) to move a cursor over a pouncing tiger in slow motion—simulating the character's ability to aim a weapon precisely—the distance sometimes becomes the element that adds friction, tension, and challenge to the moment.

Priming

Priming (or foreshadowing) involves preparing the player's mind for what to expect in the game. Most users can recall information better with visual or verbal cues, activating short-term memory associations to guide their attention. For example, you see a bunch of ammo and health on the floor before entering an unknown area; you *know* what's coming next.

Cognitive Load

How much information must a player process while playing the game? Suppose the game is too complex, with too much going on, and you must remember too much. In that case, the overwhelming mental effort required can lead to cognitive overload and an unenjoyable experience. Imagine needing to remember where your squad mates are, their status, the enemies, the missile launch codes, different colours for loot and augmented effects, special abilities, traits, the chat feed, your friends talking in your headset, the map, the shrinking danger zone, how many bullets you have left, what's the emote button, and the crafting recipes for 70 items … it can be a bit much all at once.

Anchoring Bias

Anchoring or embedding occurs when users remember or rely heavily on the first piece of information they encounter for the rest of the experience. Players may form an initial impression of the game based on its appearance, a trailer, or the first minutes of gameplay and use that as a reference point for the rest of their experience. This bias can impact how users perceive subsequent interactions with the game, overlooking or magnifying certain aspects incorrectly. Designers must ensure that the initial experience aligns with the overall experience they want to provide going forward. In 2007's *Bioshock,* the player encounters a *Big Daddy* (one of the game's most potent enemies) in a passive way that prevents engagement. They learn it poses a severe threat for future encounters simply by witnessing its power.

Von Restorff Effect

When something stands out from the rest of the items in a group, it makes it more memorable. In traditional art, we refer to this as the anomaly. This effect can make certain elements stand out and be more memorable to the player.

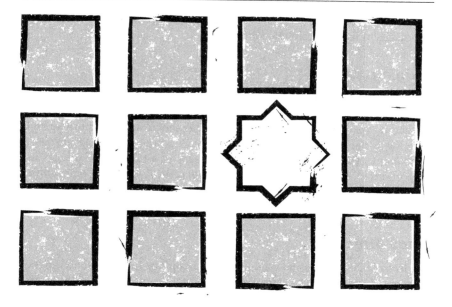

For example, essential buttons, the player's name amongst their teammates, or different inventory items can be designed to stand out from the rest of the interface or each other.

Progressive Disclosure

Progressive disclosure is a way to reduce cognitive load by gradually revealing information to players as they interact. Designers can present information or features logically and intuitively, building upon what the player has already learnt. This heuristic approach is often adopted when gradually revealing abilities to the player, sometimes via a skill tree or new weapons as they progress through the levels. Large world maps are covered in "the fog of war," and the map below is slowly revealed as the player explores.

Attentional Spotlight Effect

The attentional spotlight effect refers to our tendency to focus on specific aspects of our environment while ignoring others. We assume players can see all of the screen when playing games, but, in reality, they are shining a metaphorical spotlight on the information that gets their attention. UX designers can use this concept to direct the player's attention towards important information or actions within the game. Designers can use visual cues such as highlighting or animation to draw the player's attention. We can't assume they will see everything, and we can't direct players' attention to two competing sources of feedback simultaneously.

Nudging

Nudging involves various methods of guiding players towards specific actions or a particular path without forcing them or sometimes even allowing them to realise it. These methods can make the game feel intuitive and engaging while helping players feel they have more control and purpose. For example, the presence of law enforcement in a GTA game nudges us not to commit illegal activities. In *Overwatch* (2016), if a team composition lacked certain crucial classes, the game would nudge the players with messages stating this.

Decoy Effect

The decoy effect explains how an inferior third option, less desirable than the other two options, makes one of the original options more attractive. Game designers can use this to influence players' purchasing choices and decision-making by strategically placing a third option to steer them towards a particular choice. Designers can introduce less desirable options to make the other options look more valuable. Loot? Anyone?

Framing

Framing involves carefully selecting and presenting information to guide players towards a particular action or outcome while minimising confusion or frustration. The idea is that players are more affected by how the information is presented than the data itself. Framing can highlight important features or benefits and create urgency and desired behaviours.

Tesler's Law

Tesler's Law, also known as conservation of complexity, states that every system has a certain amount of complexity that cannot be reduced. In games, this means that the complexity of a game cannot be eliminated. Still, it can be shifted and redistributed within the game's design to make it easier for the players to use and understand. If you strip the complexity out of a game to the point where you eliminate the challenge, you also remove the fun. Equally, we shouldn't be making something superficially complex to make it seem like it has more value than it already has.

Survivorship Bias

Survivorship bias is when we fail to consider the range of outcomes and hidden evidence. People can develop a skewed view of reality. We study industry strategies and designs for successful games while overlooking those that followed the same patterns and failed. There is a trend that simply copying a successful live service game will also result in success. The postmortem of our designs doesn't account for why things fail and only focuses on what succeeds—when the failures may yield more significant data. This can lead to a skewed understanding of user preferences, as it only considers the experiences of a particular group of users who have been successful while ignoring the experiences of those who have not.

Expectation Bias

Players have preconceived expectations about the game before playing it. This can be based on marketing, reviews, or previous experience with similar games. These expectations can impact the player's experience, regardless of the actual quality of the game's features. Suppose a player expects a game to have a certain level of quality because it comes from a renowned and respected studio, but the game does not meet those expectations. In that case, the player may perceive the game as poor even if aspects of the game are well-made.

Miller's Law

Miller's law states that the human brain can only process a certain amount of information simultaneously. Specifically, it suggests that the average person can retain only about seven (plus or minus two) items in their working memory.

Meaning

Scarcity

Scarcity refers to the idea that something becomes more valuable and desirable when limited, such as rare metals, vintage collectables, or even the water and toilet paper that we'll be fighting over in post-apocalyptic wastelands of the future. This can be applied in games by creating limited-time events, rare items, or temporarily available rewards. This increases the perceived value of the reward and motivates players to engage more with the game. In role play games (RPGs), you will often find they have a colourful rarity scale on their weapons and items, ranging from common to *you-never-ever-find-this*. It can also be applied by limiting the number of lives or resources (like ammo) available to the player, making them feel more invested in the game's outcome and survival.

Curiosity Gap

The curiosity gap is a design technique that intrigues players by the game's storyline or gameplay mechanics. Creating a gap between what the player knows and wants to know entices them to continue playing. This technique is often used in games with a narrative or mystery element, where the player is given just enough information to pique their interest and keep them playing. 2016's *Firewatch* finds the player exploring and slowly unravelling a mystery in a national park in Wyoming by finding clues through the story.

Mental Model

We often enter an experience with an idea of what to expect. A mental model refers to how users perceive and understand a game based on their past experiences. Designers build a mental model throughout a game as it helps users navigate and anticipate how their actions will affect the game's outcome.

Occam's Razor

In science, we always look for the most straightforward explanation first. Simplicity is better than complexity. One of the most effective ways to manage complexity is to simplify processes and remove unnecessary steps. Our discipline has a shared philosophy that when there is no more to subtract from a design, it's nearing completion. As designers, we must analyse and consider each element, removing the unnecessary without compromising overall function.

Variable Reward

Giving the players unexpected rewards keeps them motivated to continue playing. This principle is based on the idea that humans are attracted to unpredictable rewards, which evoke excitement and anticipation—even luck. This principle is often used in games that require a lot of time and effort to complete, as it helps retain players longer. Live service and mobile games frequently trigger free rewards for returning players. *Who doesn't like free stuff?*

Survey Bias

Survey bias is particularly relevant in UX research. It refers to the distortion of survey results by influencing participants' responses. This could be the way questions are phrased, the order in which they are presented, or the demographic characteristics of the respondents. For example, if a survey only targets a specific group of players, such as hardcore gamers, the results may not accurately reflect casual gamers' or other groups' opinions and experiences.

Skeuomorphism

Skeuomorphism uses design elements that mimic real-world objects or textures within the UI. This involves using visual cues that resemble real-life objects, textures, and affordances to make the game feel more familiar and intuitive to the player. For example, the infamous cog icon represents the Settings menu, referencing the inner workings of a machine. Buttons or levers that resemble their real-life counterparts can be practical as we already know how those work.

However, overusing skeuomorphism can also lead to cluttered or confusing interfaces. It's not always fashionable, and the references are not always timely. If done poorly, it can make a UI look cheap—thus, the player's perception of that game is diminished.

Aesthetic-Usability Effect

An incorrect assumption is that appearance does not impact function. The aesthetic-usability effect states that users are more likely to overlook usability flaws in a design that looks good. Users distinguish aesthetically pleasing designs as more usable and functional than ones that are not, regardless of usability.

Cognitive Dissonance

Players feel mental discomfort when their beliefs or expectations do not match their experience. This occurs when players encounter unexpected or inconsistent elements that conflict with their preconceived notions or prior experiences. For example, if a game is marketed as a fast-paced action game but instead has slower gameplay mechanics, this may leave players frustrated or disappointed.

Time

Parkinson's Law

Like my appetite for pizza, Parkinson's law states that work expands to fill the time available for completion. In game development, if there is no set deadline or time limit for completing a task, designers may spend longer than necessary on certain elements, possibly over-engineering or causing production delays.

Investment Loops

Investment loops, also known as engagement loops or game loops, are a series of actions that keep players engaged and coming back for more. These loops are designed to create a sense of progress, reward, and achievement. Players level up their characters by playing the game, finding loot to build better loot, and then repeating the process. By creating investment loops that are both challenging and rewarding, designers can keep players engaged and invested in the game over and over again. It helps if the game is fun.

Loss Aversion

Players tend to feel the pain of losing more strongly than the joy of winning. Designers need to be careful when making challenges or obstacles in the game to ensure that players don't feel frustrated or demotivated by repeated failures. We can also apply this phenomenon to when players have gained so much and become too fearful to continue in the core gameplay. Picture yourself in a survival game, heavily armoured with top-tier loot, and high-powered weapons. Some players will avoid conflict and danger at all costs to avoid losing it all. *They stop playing the game*, and we must encourage them out of their heavily armoured shells. By understanding loss aversion, designers can establish motivations to continue participation when the stakes are high—removing the sting from loss to keep players engaged and motivated to continue.

The Sunk Cost Fallacy

Sometimes, we continue investing in something even when the outcome is no longer beneficial. Designers can see themselves continuing to invest in a feature that does not deliver a positive experience simply because they have already invested a lot of time and resources. It affects our rational decision-making. Developers must recognise when a design or feature is no longer working and be willing to let go.

Likewise, players can find themselves in a game experience where they have backed themselves into a corner and need a way out. Perhaps the game has a resource that has been squandered, and the player struggles to progress. Even simple things like a 'restart from checkpoint' are enough to get the player out of a bad run. There will always be regenerative resources to support you in building games. In Bioshock Infinite (2013), your NPC companion, Elizabeth, will throw you ammo, money, and other resources when running low.

Reactance

Players can experience negative emotions when they feel their freedom or control over the game is restricted or taken away. This can occur when the game forces them to follow a particular path or play style or limits their choices. Developers, of course, need to encourage players to do certain things and sometimes force them. In *Crysis* (2007), if the player tries to swim out into the ocean, they will be attacked by sharks; in contrast, the player character (a shark) in *Maneater* (2020) is blocked from swimming out into the open ocean by colossal fishing nets. It's okay to force the player to do something if it doesn't incite a negative emotion. The premise of 'invisible walls,' an unseen barrier that stops players from progressing to certain areas, feels cheap and lazy. Presenting a player with a legal screen is fine as long as they can get through it quickly. Forcing a player to look at something by yanking the camera away from them feels jarring and removes player agency, but encouraging them to look makes them feel more in control. Being forced to walk slowly through a dramatic segment can sometimes make the flow inconsistent. UX designers need to be aware of reactance and explain forced restrictions in a way the player accepts and allows them to make meaningful decisions on their terms.

Law of the Instrument

If given a hammer, everything becomes a nail. Designers can overly rely on familiar tools or methods, even if they are not the best fit for the task. This can lead to a lack of creativity and innovation in the design process and a failure to consider alternative solutions that may be more effective. If we keep using the same design and prototyping software, will all game user interfaces start to look similar? We should approach each new project with an open mind and explore a variety of new and existing tools and techniques to find the best solution for the specific experience.

In games, this can be used to our advantage. If you give the player a hammer and everything becomes a nail, why not roll with it? This could lead to fun gameplay and encourage players to interact organically with their surroundings. If the player has a gun, they will probably try to shoot everything. Some VR games require players to use their weapons to eliminate enemies and interact with menus.

Temptation Bundling

This principle uses game elements such as rewards, incentives, and challenges to encourage players to keep playing or complete an objective. Temptation bundling combines a desirable activity with a less desirable one to make the latter more enjoyable. This might involve integrating tasks, such as grinding or levelling up, with more pleasurable activities, such as exploring new areas or engaging in combat.

Decision Fatigue

Players experience mental exhaustion when constantly required to make decisions. When presented with too many choices or complex decision-making tasks, they may become overwhelmed and start to make less rational decisions, or stop caring. Designers must be mindful of the number and complexity of players' decisions to avoid decision fatigue and ensure that players remain engaged and motivated.

Weber-Fechner Laws

Our experiences are made up of stimuli that activate all our senses—vision, hearing, taste, touch, and smell. A person's ability to distinguish between two stimuli depends on the magnitude of those stimuli. In games (where we don't have taste or smell yet), players adapt better to small incremental changes. For example, a small button scaling to a slightly bigger button is noticeable. However, a large button scaling the proportional same amount won't be. A pistol may vibrate the gamepad slightly, but a bazooka must rattle the gamepad to be perceived as more powerful.

Affect Heuristic

The affect heuristic is a psychological concept explaining how people rely on their emotions and feelings when making judgements or decisions rather than using logic or reason. It applies to UX because players' emotional responses can heavily impact their overall experience and enjoyment. For example, players may feel negatively towards a game with frustrating mechanics or a confusing interface, even if it has good graphics or exciting storylines. On the other hand, a game with intuitive controls and satisfying feedback can evoke positive emotions and enhance the player's experience.

This concept is also valid when conducting interviews and surveys. Participants' current emotions can cloud their judgement and impact the data received. Before conducting interviews and user tests, researchers should conduct well-being assessments to determine the subject's emotional state, as this may factor into how reliable the data is before the results are gathered. If a user has recently experienced something that has elicited a negative emotion, they may be overly critical or struggle to remain objective.

IKEA Effect

The IKEA effect is not the feeling you get after leaving Ikea with a belly full of meatballs and a trolley full of items when you only went in for a spatula. It refers to the tendency for people to value things more highly when they have contributed to their creation. In UX, players feel more invested in a game they have helped create or customise. If a game allows players to customise their characters, weapons, or buildings, they may feel a sense of ownership and attachment to their creation.

Memory and Learning

Heuristic principles are designated to enable someone to discover or learn. This is important in games as it negates the constant need for repetitive reminders and tutorials for repeated actions. Things begin to feel intuitive because we have learnt something; frankly, it's much more fun.

Cognitive Load

Wait, didn't we cover this already?

Sensory Appeal

Developers can enhance the gaming experience by engaging players through sight, sound, vibrant colours, dynamic sound effects, smooth animations, and tactile feedback. It also makes elements more accessible when they are not solely reliant on one form of stimuli. You can't just present feedback in a colour change. *Yes, I am glad you made the thing red, but I can't see red.* Allowing players to customise the presentation or amount of stimulation allows for better accessibility and usability. For example, vibration sucks for players with conditions such as RSI/carpal tunnel, which can cause physical pain. The game becomes unplayable when it cannot be toggled off or reduced in the game settings.

Endowment Effect

The endowment effect is a cognitive bias where people value something more once they own it. This means they are more likely to overvalue something they have compared to something they have not. Players are more likely to value features or aspects of the game they have already experienced or used. For example, if a player is used to a particular navigation system, they may resist change to it, even if the new system is objectively better. UX designers need to be aware of this bias and find ways to introduce new features or changes that don't trigger this effect or at least minimise its impact. This can be done by gradually introducing new features and providing clear benefits. Ownership can also factor into how players can customise elements. Adding custom names to guns, cities, theme parks, or digital pets has more perceived value and connection with players. Losing my first horse 'Noodle' in *Red Dead Redemption Two* (2018) was a sad day indeed.

Delighters

Delighters refer to the unexpected elements that add an extra layer of enjoyment to their experience. These can be micro details like character animations, sound effects, or easter eggs that surprise and delight. They enhance the player's emotional experience and make the game more memorable. A game could include hidden levels, humorous dialogue, bonus content, being able to pet an animal, or anything "meme-able" that can create a sense of excitement, keeping the user engaged and elevating their experience.

Recognition > Recall

Recognition is greater than recall because it is easier for players to recognise something they have seen or done than recall it from memory. When users encounter a familiar element in a game, such as a button or icon, they quickly understand its purpose and how to interact with it. Still, it can be more challenging if users have to recall information from memory. Some controls are so habitual, like the Select and Start buttons or triggers in a shooter, that experienced players inherently know how to operate the basics of a game or menu immediately. By favouring a recognition-based design, developers can make their games more intuitive and user-friendly.

Negativity Bias

In games, negativity bias can play a significant role in shaping a player's overall experience. Negative experiences, emotions, and information are recalled and more significantly impact a person's psychological state than positive ones. If a game has frustrating mechanics or design flaws that cause negative emotions, players are likelier to dwell on those experiences rather than the positive ones.

Goal-Gradient Effect

The closer people reach their goal, the more motivated they become to achieve it. This effect can create a sense of progress and provide users with clear information about their advancement. This can be achieved using progress bars, quest lists, objective HUDS, scoreboards, or other visual indicators showing users how far they are from completing a level or achieving a specific objective. This makes users more likely to become motivated to keep playing the game. Making it look exciting even when incomplete is an excellent way to improve motivation.

Peak-end Rule

This principle suggests people judge an experience based on two key moments: the most intense point (peak) and how it ends. In UX, we focus on creating memorable and joyous moments during gameplay and when interacting with interfaces. This makes players more likely to remember the game positively and want to return to play again. Identify what peak areas produce the most joy, provide the best experience, and highlight those accordingly.

Serial Position Effect

People are more likely to remember the first and last items in a list, not those in the middle. UX designers must pay attention to information placement. By placing important information or tasks at the beginning or end of a list, designers can improve the chances that players will recognise and engage with them.

Doherty Threshold

The Doherty threshold principle established the objective of keeping users engaged when interacting with a computer. According to a study in the late 1970s, users eventually become disinterested if a response appears after the 400 ms threshold. Designers can help reduce the frustration by keeping response times under the 400 ms threshold. If this is unavoidable, designers must provide feedback to negate disengagement. In games, especially on mobile devices, if you're waiting for a level to load or finalising the purchase of some gems, provide some feedback to maintain engagement as the processes complete. You may be able to play the game a little bit and practise some moves whilst the level loads.

Postel's Law

Postel's law, also known as the robustness principle, states, "Be conservative in what you do; be liberal in what you accept from others." In other words, when designing a system, one should be strict about what is sent out, but we must be forgiving and flexible in how we accept input from the player. This means that the UI should be able to handle a wide range of input, even if it is not exactly what was expected. For example, if the player accidentally presses the wrong button or inputs the wrong command, the UI should be able to recover and provide feedback to the player on what went wrong and how to correct it.

Jakob's Law

"Those who cannot remember the past are condemned to repeat it" – *George Santayana.*

Users expect a level of consistency and familiarity across all websites and applications. We are used to seeing specific design patterns and layouts, and when we encounter something new, we may have difficulty navigating or understanding it. Designers should aim to create interfaces that share some consistency with other games in the same genre or with similar gameplay mechanics. This is not to say we shouldn't innovate when the status quo is no longer adequate. There is nothing wrong with a designer going to the fantastic *GameUIDatabase.com* and looking at how other games work.

Default Bias

Players can sometimes stick with the default option, even if it's not their best choice. Players may favour the path of least resistance, and the challenge encourages them to try new approaches. To combat this, designers must ensure that alternative options are discoverable, desirable, and easily accessible. This can be achieved by highlighting the benefits, providing clear instructions and explanations, and offering rewards and incentives.

GESTALT THEORY AND VISUAL PERCEPTION

Gestalt theory is an approach to understanding how humans perceive objects visually. Take a basketball. The first thing we perceive is its shape—a sphere. Then, we note its colour. After that, we notice its form, pattern, texture, lines, and text. It may happen in a split second, but humans perceive things linearly. Our brains unconsciously use cues like these to decide what the ball is, hopefully before it hits us in the face.

The elements of an image include internal paths, forces, and energies that are not immediately obvious but are subconsciously perceived. These elements guide our attention towards focal areas within the image that hold greater significance. As a result, hierarchies form, and connections are established.

Our brains try to group elements in an organised, simple, and meaningful way, even when the parts are separate entities. Designers who grasp these principles can develop more effective designs, layouts, and visual language that better engage their target audience.

Several key psychological ideas exist behind Gestalt theory. The concept of **emergence** explores the formation of complex patterns from simple rules. In design, it is crucial to identify elements by their general form and balance simplicity and detail. Additionally, **reification** involves transforming abstract ideas into tangible concepts by filling informational gaps. This process often relies on familiar patterns, even if they are not an exact match. **Multi-stability** refers to the experience of perceiving something in multiple interpretations, leading to constant switches in perception. Lastly, **invariance** highlights our ability to recognise similarities and differences in simple objects, regardless of size, rotation, or position.

The Gestalt Principles

Proximity

Humans perceive objects that are near each other as grouped. When they are closer together, organising related elements and separating unrelated elements help users quickly and easily identify related information. In an interface, we can indicate which elements are menu options, game controls, or character statistics, making it easier for players to locate the information they need.

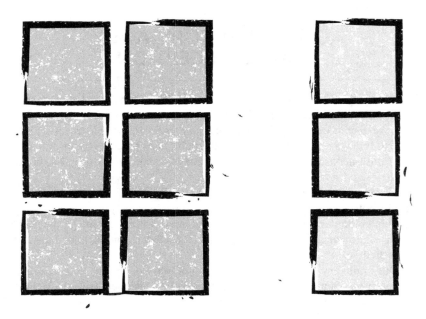

Similarity

Objects with similar attributes are perceived as related or grouped. Similar colours, shapes, and styles are used for components with similar functions or purposes, for example, making all the heroes' combat ability icons spikey orange hexagons, while the magic ability icons are all glowing purple diamonds.

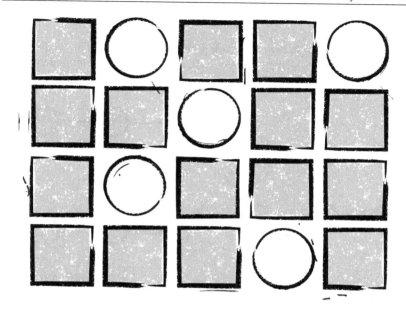

Common Region

People tend to group elements when enclosed within a common boundary. In UI design, panels, overlays, lines, shapes, or colours group related elements and separate them from unrelated ones.

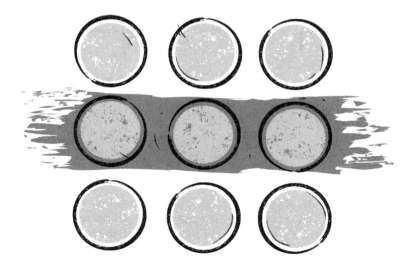

Continuity

Elements aligned with each other are perceived as related. This helps users understand the relationships between different components and makes navigating the interface more accessible.

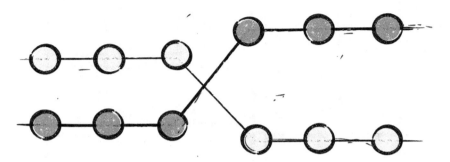

Closure

The human brain completes incomplete shapes by filling in the missing information. This means that even if a shape is not entirely closed, our brain perceives it as complete. By using incomplete shapes, designers can create a sense of movement and dynamism. A dashed line in the shape of a circle will still look like a circle, even with large gaps between the dashes. Sometimes, this practice is adopted in vertical or horizontal list boxes where half of the last visible option is faded to imply further options if you keep scrolling.

Figure Ground

Humans are naturally wired to distinguish between a foreground (figure) and a background. Designers should ensure that critical information or elements are visually contrasted with their surroundings to make them easier to notice.

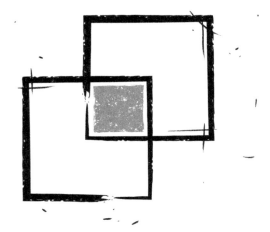

Uniform Connectedness

Visually connected elements are perceived as a single group in the user's mind. Using the same style for all the buttons in a game can help users understand that they are all part of the same interface and perform related functions. Menu buttons are often stacked together so players have some idea of what those interactions do by association.

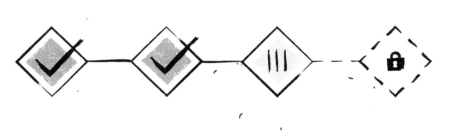

Common Fate

People perceive objects that move or change similarly as more related or connected. Items that animate or change at the same time are considered related. It's hard to show this in a still image.

Prägnanz (Simplicity)

People identify ambiguous or complex images and simplify them to reduce cognitive effort. Think about how you used to draw houses as a kid. Maybe you still draw houses the same now?

UX PRINCIPLES

User-Centricity

If it isn't evident by now, UX is about the people. It means putting the target user's needs, preferences, and experiences at the forefront of the design process. However, we're not just making a game for the player. We still aim to create innovation or an artistic vision and deliver an influential social message or a new story. Innovation, creative expression, and technology drive momentum in design and give UX designers the vital task of re-establishing the experience time and time again. If games were made just for the player, based on market research, we would be back at the whole *"just add more horses"* scenario.

Games are designed to have challenges (friction), whilst apps are designed to make tasks require less effort. User-centricity involves creating experiences that prioritise user satisfaction, engagement, and enjoyment. The aim is to understand the target audience and integrate their feedback and insights into the game development process. Understanding player preferences, conducting playtesting and feedback, ensuring personalisation and accessibility, and fostering community engagement are vital elements in creating immersive and successful gaming experiences.

Consistency

Consistency is the fundamental principle of maintaining a uniform approach throughout the game. This means the UI should stay consistent in aesthetics, interaction, and functionality. This helps users feel comfortable and generates value. They understand how to navigate the game's mechanics and find what they need quickly, as they have built a heuristic understanding of what has been laid out before them.

Feedback

The player needs clear and immediate information about their actions and inactions. This information can be visual, auditory, or haptic (preferably a combination) to help understand their actions. It allows players to learn and improve their skills and keeps them engaged. Good feedback should be timely, relevant, and unambiguous.

Equitable Use

A product must be designed to be usable by people with diverse abilities without further adaptation or specialised design. Significant efforts must be made to ensure the game is accessible to those with temporary or situational impairments, as well as to players with visual, auditory, physical, or cognitive disabilities.

Affordance

Affordance refers to the perceived possibility of an action that an object or environment offers based on real-world understanding. *It looks like what I think it should do.* For example, a door handle needs pulling or pushing, and a big red button needs pressing. People inherently know this information.

Hierarchy

Hierarchy is the organisation and prioritisation of information in a way that guides the user's attention and helps them understand importance, structure, and flow. Visual cues, such as colour, size, and placement, communicate the essentials, the actions they can take, and what the consequences will be.

Conceptual Model

A conceptual model is an abstract, psychological representation of how designers want users to perform tasks. Through some form or another created by the designers (be it documentation, tutorials, guides, or systemically based on their interactions), players intuitively build a model of how something should work in their minds, hopefully aligning with the designer's way of thinking. Conceptual models are crucial in games to map out logical activities the player can do, so they understand how to navigate the world, UI, mechanics, and controls together.

Error Prevention and Tolerance for Error

Error prevention involves reducing the likelihood of errors occurring from the outset. In games, this can include concise instructions, forgiving text input forms, intuitive controls, and helpful feedback.

Tolerance for error refers to how well a product or system can handle errors when they occur to avoid frustration and discouragement. This can include providing multiple ways to complete a task and allowing players to undo their actions. If you accidentally sell a rare sword to an old, crusty merchant, there will usually be a mechanic to let you get it back after the transaction is concluded.

Low Physical Effort

When designing games, we must minimise the physical effort required to interact with them, thus reducing the risk of physical discomfort or injury from prolonged use. This involves ensuring players can easily navigate menus, controls, and gameplay mechanics without exerting themselves by implementing intuitive control schemes, ergonomic button layouts, and streamlined menu interfaces. We also avoid including actions such as button holds or repeated button taps that might cause discomfort or be impossible for players with physical limitations or impairments. Accessible design is a crucial consideration in this principle.

Constraints

A constraint, restriction, or limitation, by definition, sounds like a negative thing. However, boundaries give us an idea of what space we have to work with. Designers with constraints can think openly inside set parameters and focus on what matters most. For example, a complex game with numerous actions must still work with a gamepad limited to a few buttons.

Keep It Simple, Stupid! (K.I.S.S.)

Designs work best when they are kept simple. Creating a *Rube Goldberg-style machine* design won't help anyone. Ask yourself why it needs to be so complicated. Am I doing this for me? Simple does not mean dull. Try to remember who you are making this for.

Remind yourself to keep it simple, stupid.

NOTE

---

1   bbc.co.uk/newsround/54823446

UX
Not UI

5

DESIGN STAGES

Stay with me on this. Imagine UI as a car. The wheels, seats, and buttons are the interface. The engine, gears, and electronics are all logic and programming. UX is all these elements plus the reason we need the car in the first place. It's how we know how to drive and how we feel once we are inside. Now that we understand the theory and principles that drive UX, let's delve into the processes behind how it's all put into gear.

Studios vary in scale, values, and resources. Each has a distinct culture around UX, and every team composition is different. Some studios don't even have one. Processes vary, and things aren't always within your control, so don't expect every studio to work similarly.

Research and Planning

Before diving in, it's crucial to understand your target audience. In this critical stage, you will discover your players' identities and needs and define the game's objectives, mechanics, and competition.

Concept and Ideation

After establishing our research, we explore ideas through brainstorming, prototypes, low-fidelity wireframes, initial stakeholder feedback, and surveying early assumptions. Some ideas become potential solutions; others are

DOI: 10.1201/9781003367116-5

discarded. Multiple design proposals are generated and refined to the most practical and innovative solutions.

Design and Production

As production ramps up, development intensifies. The UX team will focus on the final features, collaborating with other disciplines like UI and programming.

Testing and Iteration

Features are tested with users throughout the various stages of production. Teams review the feedback, and necessary adjustments are made.

Launch and Post-launch

Good news, everyone! The game has launched and is available to the public! By releasing the game, you're expanding your testing pool, allowing more time for feedback, data analysis, and discovering and resolving new challenges with each update.

RESEARCH

How to conduct effective research:

1. Identify and align your focus with the project's values, creating a clear roadmap.
2. Construct the right questions. Use "what" for exploring features, "how" for processes, and "why" for motivations. Aim for one idea per question, and use concise language to obtain rich, usable data. Be mindful of biases that can skew results and prioritise questions based on project impact and ease of implementation. Pilot test all your questions to eliminate poor ones and iterate by refining your questions based on early results.
3. Provide evaluation options to improve and ground your research in data.

Competitive Analysis

Now, I am not suggesting you don a ski mask and rappel into a rival corporate HQ—there is an easier way. In UX, competitive analysis involves appraising similar games to gain insights into best practices, trends, strengths, weaknesses, and audience expectations. Remember *Jakob's law*.

Motivational Models

To create motivational models, we typically consider what motivations we intend to target in the game. We determine which motivations to combine to make the game more engaging and appealing to a larger audience. By analysing different motivational groups, we can build models to better understand the target audience.

This process involves identifying user motivations such as:

- action
- completion
- creativity
- fantasy
- power

- achievement
- immersion
- mastery
- story
- social interaction

This knowledge helps define user personas and tailor the game to better meet the expectations of its intended audience.

Player Experience Goals

Player experience goals are desired outcomes for players. They guide the decision-making process and are used to create goals that use the same language as our motivations, for example, *fantasy, power, community,* and *challenge.*

Goal: Players will feel like a team of real superheroes when they use their unique abilities to fight off waves of enemies within the time limit.

Can you see how this goal relates to motivation? *"Players," "community,"* and *"team"* satisfy our social goal while being flexible enough for designers to make them competitive if desired. The premise that you feel like a *"real superhero"* implies the player will live the hero *fantasy* and that there will be different types of heroes. Open terms such as "special abilities" and "time limit" allow the goal to link to *power* and *challenge.*

Well-phrased goals help narrow the focus, making them measurable while still allowing freedom for the developers to explore and iterate within these constraints.

User Interview

User interviews gain insight into players' behaviour, preferences, and pain points. They can be conducted in person, online, or over the phone and are used to inform design decisions, such as what features to include or focus on, how to structure the game, and how to bring about various UX improvements.

Empathy Map

Empathy maps help us understand users' feelings, thoughts, and behaviours. They consist of four quadrants, considering what the users see, hear, feel, and do. This information is used to create personas to expose where their needs are unmet.

User Personas

Personas are fictional representations of a specific type of user within the target audience. Each is based on research and data and includes information about typical users' goals, needs, behaviours, and preferences. Multiple personas representing specific needs and extremes from the target user group are preferable. We use these personas in our language to anchor our decisions based on people rather than assumptions or preferences, allowing for more informed decisions on features, structure, and communication.

How to create user personas:

1. Conduct thorough research on your target audience and gather information through surveys, interviews, or focus groups
2. Analyse your findings to identify patterns and insights to help define them
3. Determine the demographic information, goals, motivations, pain points, and behaviours
4. Bring your user persona to life by creating a profile with a name, picture, and critical information about the "person"
5. Test your user persona with real users and refine it based on feedback to ensure it accurately represents your target audience

6. Continue to iterate and refine as you learn more. This process helps link your user persona to competitive analysis and motivational models.

Journey Mapping

Journey mapping visualises and understands all the stages of a player's voyage, from initial awareness to final satisfaction. This technique helps identify pain points, technical constraints, and opportunities for improvement. Creating these can be a headache, especially if the overall game design is incomplete, so work closely with stakeholders to ensure the design accurately reflects the vision. Use whatever software you like and can afford. Some paid-for programmes have better quality-of-life features and collaborative support, but you can find free versions with the same features and do the job just as well.

ACCESSIBLE DESIGN

Suppose we jump back to our car analogy. When we enter a new car, we all adjust the seat, the mirrors, the air conditioning, and the music to suit our preferences. It's the same car for each of us, and the challenge of driving is the same, but if you can't adjust the seat to reach the pedals, you can't enjoy the drive. Games are no different. The challenge for a gamer should be the gameplay, something they *can* control, not something they can't.

Our needs vary based on physical or cognitive conditions. Others are situational or temporary (e.g., playing a game with your sleeping baby on your lap or having a broken wrist). Some come with our comprehension of language, age, or capability. Understanding the audience's needs is a crucial aspect of accessible design, making them feel understood and valued. You might not think you need any accessibility features right now, but as we age, we all do in some way. You may use accessible features all the time and not even think of it in that way, and that's the point. By incorporating accessible principles, developers can ensure that a broad audience enjoys their games inclusively. This empowerment allows us to overcome challenges we can't control, making the game more enjoyable and putting us in the driver's seat of our gaming experience.

Accessibility Is for Everyone

Economically, it expands the game's market reach. According to industry statistics, there will be nearly 3 billion gamers worldwide by 2029, and studies estimate individuals with disabilities make up around 20% to 45% of the gaming population[1]. The potential audience is vast, and they'll welcome any game they can play (anyone from publishing/marketing, remember to post your accessibility features before release, so people know if they can play before purchase). More importantly, it's a step towards equity and ensures everyone can benefit from the joy video games provide. Games are experiences, distractions, and, for many, an escape. Accessibility isn't about overcoming the challenges in people's lives; it's about removing those challenges from the equation.

To adequately explain accessible design, we need to make a few critical distinctions.

- **Difficulty** is relative. Accessibility is not *making the game easier* or *babying the player.*
- **Capability** is one's ability to overcome game challenges.
- **Barriers** prevent people from overcoming game challenges. Everyone wants game challenges; without them, there is nothing to do, learn, or overcome. These are intentional barriers; unintentional barriers are put up without designers even realising it.
- **Disability** is the mismatch between someone's capability and a barrier. Someone isn't disabled because they use a wheelchair and can't get upstairs but because no mechanism enables them to avoid stairs.
- **Accessibility** is the mechanism that eliminates the mismatch between capability and the barrier.

We essentially prohibit players from playing when encountering an intentional or unintentional barrier. Accessible design resolves these barriers and promotes inclusivity (making people not feel inferior for encountering those barriers).

Three approaches to dealing with a barrier:

1. Like everyone else, players can be given tools to **penetrate** a barrier to progress. These include button/key remapping, screen readers, aim-assist, colour-blind support, text adjustments, subtitles, and audio cues.

2. Players can **go around** a barrier by creating an alternative path, for instance, adding branching paths, diverse gameplay mechanics (like swapping repeat button presses for holds or single presses), and providing different playstyles and game modes.
3. Players can **skip** the wall and overly challenging segments entirely. Though not an ideal solution, sometimes it's the only viable way not to block the entire experience, which is a worse outcome. Sometimes, barriers can be dull or repetitive, and all gamers appreciate avoiding them. *GTA V* (2013) would let players skip missions after failing three times, and for most of the series, you could skip the duration of a taxi ride to reach the destination quicker—if only we could do that in real life. These are useful for non-core gameplay events and elements, like skipping quick-time events (QTEs), adjusting difficulty settings mid-game, or automatically adjusting mechanics to simplify them.

It is also essential to consider a more inclusive use of language. Do the research and use the correct terminology. Avoid using words like "disabled" for option labels. Be creative when naming your difficulty levels, so people do not feel degraded for picking a lower level of challenge suitable for their capability. What is "normal"? What's deemed "easy" to you might be a challenge to someone else, and that challenge may not be in their control. *Star Wars Jedi: Fallen Order* (2019) named their challenge levels using language in canon with the intellectual property (IP), and *The Last of Us Part II* (2020) broke up their difficulty screen into categories (enemies, resources, etc.) so players could adjust each challenge level for a truly tailored experience.

The least practical approach is to 'tag on' accessibility features at the end of production. Maintaining this substandard approach leads to more challenging implementations, ineffective compromises, and crucial features falling away. It's far easier to build accessibility into the conversation early and include it in your design process. Accessibility is an opportunity for innovation; you might not even need new features if there is no barrier to overcome.

IDEATION AND PRODUCTION

UX work continues even after a product has been released. We must consider the users' needs with every new addition and iteration. However, not all of these processes are done by a UX designer, depending on the studio. Understanding these procedures will help you appreciate their value in game production.

Information Architecture

Information architecture (IA) is about creating a logical and intuitive structure for game content that aligns with a user's mental model and expectations. It's organising and structuring content to make it easy to find, understand, and use. This includes creating a clear and concise hierarchy, using consistent labelling, and grouping similar elements. Presenting information in order of importance but making essential elements more prominent helps people gain information faster and improves aesthetics.

User Flow

A user flow chart or diagram maps out the path a player takes to complete a task in a game. They can be used to illustrate how they will navigate menus or specific interactions. Designers can establish when to present the correct information and allow players to complete desired tasks in as few steps as possible. These visual aids help plan features and technical requirements.

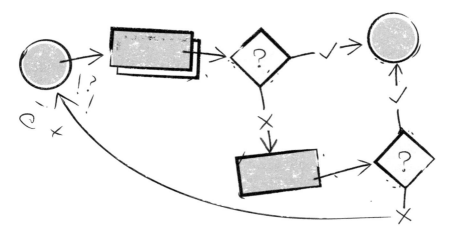

Interaction Design

Interaction is the language between two things. A dialogue between humans and technology is known as human-computer interaction (HCI). It focuses explicitly on encouraging smooth and effortless connections while ensuring the usage is functional, efficient, and enjoyable. Interaction design helps create mechanics, controls, and interface elements, ensuring players can intuitively interact with these features. A well-designed interaction can be the difference between a game that is frustrating to play and one that is accessible, engaging, and challenging for the right reasons.

Every interaction gives players more information. It's an intentionally heuristic approach, where the players gradually learn, become independent, and eventually embed themselves into the game's ecosystem. Gamers often enter a new game with existing knowledge but must relearn something new, the "rules of engagement," even if they seem mostly familiar. It's similar to when you upgrade your phone—how you feel like a novice when starting a new game (even with simple things like operating familiar-looking menus) and then later becoming an expert.

Good Rules for Interactions

Ensure Consistency and Clarity
Implementing a clear and consistent design language should ensure the player knows how and what to interact with. It would be best to avoid situations where your players are *relearning* how to interact with similar things. Create an interaction guide for your project to define each interaction type and where it is appropriate to use. Maintain and update it as needed for easy team reference.

Keep It Simple, Stupid (K.I.S.S.)
Yes, this again. Reduce the jargon. Assume they have never experienced something like this before. No one has played *this* game.

Make Things Obvious
Avoid hiding your interactions in obscurity unless it's like a super-secret 'easter egg.' If your interactions are related to movement in specific directions, indicate that in some capacity. Considering *Jakob's law* again, there is nothing wrong with conforming to what players might expect based on past titles. Familiar interactions are something you can highlight in your competitive analysis.

Rely on Recognition
Humans look for familiarity. Particular objects and shapes have meanings we recognise. Where possible, give your interactions some affordance.

Set the Tone
Your interactions need to be suitable for the game you are making. We don't want to patronise and pander or be too complex either. The tone must be consistent throughout the experience to avoid feeling jarring and disjointed.

Feedback

Feedback is crucial. How do you know when you have done something correctly or can't interact at all? The result is obvious when you transition to another screen or lift the car off trapped civilians. But what about "micro-interactions"? Small, momentary interactions that don't result in a massive change are just as helpful and tantalising as the more significant ones. Even the slightest hint stops an action from feeling unresponsive and produces the clarity a player needs. Feedback can come in many forms, from subtle colour changes and sounds to rambunctious translations (movement), vibration, and eye-gouging effects.

UX Writing

UX writing defines the 'copy' (content like text, diagrams, and images) within a UI to guide and help users. Like the beginning of a captivating book, engaging UX writing breathes life into content, ignites excitement, and creates curiosity. It's imperative because it allows players to understand game mechanics, objectives, and critical feedback in an approachable way. This may include tutorials, item descriptions, instructions, prompts, and pop-ups that appear during gameplay.

We're not writing sterile instructions, but using simple language is crucial. It's about being authentic, encouraging, and connecting in a relatable way. Our writing should be aimed at the target audience and accessible to newcomers. These elements must be meticulously created to ensure engagement and enhance immersion, helping players stay motivated throughout the game.

UX Writing Best Practises

Brevity

Whether diving into an action-packed gaming world or immersing in a story-driven adventure, gamers crave clear information. Ensure your sentences are concise and remain on target. Speak like a human. Ensure the message is the priority when injecting flavour and narrative into objectives, descriptions, and biographies, while keeping any system information straightforward. For example:

"WARNING! No Controller has been detected as connected, Mighty Explorer. Please re-insert your controller into your console to resume your gaming experience post-haste!"

To:

"Controller Disconnected: Please reconnect your controller."

Don't Blame the Player

Instead of just telling them they made a mistake, help them correct it. This is a teaching moment, not a blame game.

Consider Tone and Voice

The voice of your writing needs to match the tone of your game. Your writing should be more formal if it's a serious game, and light-hearted if it is a playful one.

Avoid Double Negatives

It doesn't not get confusing.

> "Choosing higher settings is not insignificant in its impact on performance."

To:

> "Choosing higher settings can significantly impact performance."

Be Helpful

Something like *"More info"* on a prompt callout is vague. *"Preview Item"* or *"Play Video"* gives the player more engaging insight.

Don't Be Generic

Change *"Start Game"* to *"Raise the Anchor!"* or *"Set Sail"* (if it's a pirate game, obviously). However, this can get confusing if you do it for every option.

Use Numbers Instead of Writing Numbers as Words

It saves space and is easier 2 understand... *No, wait. That doesn't look right.*
    Using actual digits instead of spelling out numbers is more precise and saves space, especially in large bodies of text.

XP Level 42 > XP Level Forty-Two
42 DMG > Forty-Two DMG
4242 Points > Four Thousand Two Hundred and Forty-Two Points!

Use an Active Voice

Active language is more engaging and can help players feel more involved in the game. Use action verbs and avoid passive voice to make your writing more dynamic. In simpler terms:

- Object + Verb + Subject = *Passive Voice*
- Subject + Verb + Object = *Active Voice*

> "This outfit can be customised by you."

To:

> "You can customise this outfit."

Consider your first words

Get to the point.

> "You are about to return to the main menu. Any unsaved data will be lost. Continue?"

To:

> "Returning to the main menu, any unsaved data will be lost. Continue?"

Picking the right prepositions

A preposition shows the relationship between a noun or pronoun and other words in a sentence. To pick the correct preposition, it's essential to understand the context and meaning of the sentence. It might seem trivial, but small things in UX have a significant impact.

> "Sync your profile to multiple platforms."

To:

> "Sync your profile across multiple platforms."

Punctuation

Punctuation has specific nuances when writing comprehensive text for interfaces. Although it generally conforms to the rules of the particular language it's written in, punctuation is often simplified in games to provide better readability, hierarchy, and text scanning.

It's unnecessary to use full stops all the time. For example, you would not need a full stop in headers/titles, buttons, labels, hints, incomplete sentences, bullet points, and single lines of body text. Still, they are needed in body text with multiple sentences and paragraphs. Due to the nature of video games, exclamation points are often used! As expected, question marks are used for questions, confirmations to the player, and to annoy Batman.

Wireframes

A wireframe is a visual representation of the UI. It shows the organisation and placement of information and interactions without aesthetic elements such as colours, images, or typography. It's essentially a blueprint, providing technical information for designers, artists, and engineers. It's also the first stage in testing assumptions and getting stakeholder approval. Wireframes continue to be used in different stages of the design process. There are two types of wireframes: low-fidelity and high-fidelity.

Low-fidelity wireframes are basic rough sketches, with literally no artwork. They are not intended to wow or provide any pizazz whatsoever; they are, in fact, flavourless. They aim to communicate the 'big idea' rather than get lost in the details. They are created quickly to establish content requirements and basic layouts, convey ideas, allow collaboration, and experiment with assumptions.

High-fidelity wireframes, on the other hand, are detailed and polished. They contain more elements, utilise actual content data, and use specific interface design patterns.

If you use just one of these tools and processes listed in this chapter, make it a wireframe. You'll need a plan before you start, even if it's sketched onto a humble scrap of paper.

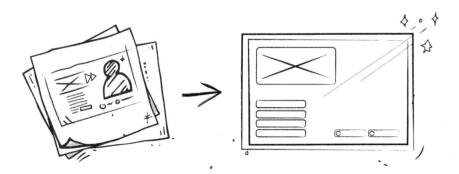

Digital Prototype

There's no substitute for putting an interactive example into someone's hand. Whether interactive or not, a prototype is a tangible representation of the final game's functionality and feel. More importantly, it's a tool for gathering feedback. It's the quickest way to gauge if something feels right and allows people to experience its effectiveness more successfully. By testing the game early on with a digital prototype, UX designers can collect insights from the team and users, enabling them to make necessary adjustments and enhance the UX. Given the high cost of production time, this isolated exploration can significantly reduce wasteful iteration.

It's sometimes difficult to predict the level of imagination your audience has when reviewing a wireframe. I once had a director say a wireframe was *too grey and dull*. If you want an idea to prevail, you must give it the opportunity to succeed. This means adjusting the quality bar based on the intended audience. I could show another designer a scrap of paper idea, and they'd get it immediately, but suppose you are presenting to a stakeholder who may not be too knowledgeable about the design process. In this case, you may want to increase the fidelity as they may not understand the inferred parts or your general idea. This is when a prototype comes into its own and helps those less able to imagine how something will work.

Onboarding

Onboarding introduces new players to the game and helps them understand its mechanics, objectives, and rules. The primary goal is to immerse players in the gameplay as quickly as possible without compromising their enjoyment. This process typically involves tutorials, tooltips, and other forms of guidance. In the past, a player would insert a coin, press start, and be thrust into the game. Today, we start the FTUE (first-time user experience) before the player leaps over obstacles and smashes up zombies. However, onboarding remains a relevant requirement for new features encountered later in the game.

The first five minutes of any game are critical. The FTUE assists players through those first five minutes until we feel they can start playing without impairing their enjoyment, gameplay knowledge, and, ultimately, lasting opinion of the game. FTUE is not just a menu screen sequence the player interacts with before starting a game; it extends into the initial gameplay and is revisited whenever we re-introduce something new.

These first interactions establish the player's needs, and they can often start with determining if the player needs audial assistance, with all UI text options being converted to synthesised speech. Following this, players will be given options to adjust their preferences before starting the game and tutorials to prevent spoiling initial understanding, enjoyment, and immersion. Nothing can ruin the start of a game faster than missing the opening story because players can't turn on subtitles (which should be on by default) until after the game's first cutscene or when they are unable to adjust PC graphics settings right away, making it feel like they're playing on a potato.

As an industry, we must put a stop to tiresome tutorials. We must stop forcing the player to parrot the moves called out to them or read vast blocks of text with multiple button prompts to remember. We must strive to make them fun and engaging so the lessons can sink in. Try adding some context and some narrative. *Helldivers 2* (2024) has one of the most incredible tutorials I've ever played. It was fun, memorable, and incredibly tongue-in-cheek, perfect for the game's tone. However, if you wrote it down on paper, it may sound generic and contrived, but the comedy and presentation sold it. You felt like a snot-nosed cadet, with rushed basic training as you were fed to the meat grinder. It felt amusing and engaging as you learnt the basic controls and game loop and how to have fun with them.

If you have ever played Insomniac's *Spider-Man* games, you know how exciting it is to start the game, suddenly plummeting from the top of a sky-scraper into the open-world playground of New York City. As you hang in the air for a split second, the game slows down and presents you with a single call to action—*press to swing*. This exhilarating feeling instantly washes over you and lingers. You are now Spider-Man! The superhero fantasy is fulfilled immediately. The designers decided to literally drop new players from the top of a building, much like a mother bird teaching her young to fly. It's no wonder these games are so loved by fans of the superhero genre!

Making a great FTUE requires some creativity. It's not about bombarding players with all the available options the game supports, as this can be overwhelming. We must get them started in a way that suits them and be selective with what is essential in the moment.

Effective Game UX

Achieving great UX is not an exact science. Every experience has different requirements and different people. Don't assume you know what the players want: *you are not the user.*

Collect feedback, do research, and validate what players wish to do. Remember:

- Predictable functionality improves usability and reduces errors; people don't need to keep learning how things work

- Difficulty is not linear
- Balance realism with gameplay
- Don't overdo tutorials
- The first five minutes are critical
- Recognise micro-interactions
- Narrative feedback is more meaningful
- Accessibility is inclusive
- Don't silo UX decisions within the team
- Never overwhelm players with too much information or too many options
- Don't iterate without testing
- Don't redesign for the sake of it; not everything needs redoing
- Players only like change if something doesn't work or they ask for it. Don't do it if there are no clear goals
- Keep changes small to prevent shocking players

TESTING

Usability Test

Usability testing evaluates a game or an isolated part by trialling it with real users. Playtests provide valuable feedback to help identify problem areas and successful implementations. Players' feedback is gathered to assess if the design intent is achieved and if the feature is intuitive, efficient, and satisfies the needs. Several factors must be considered when conducting a practical usability test.

First, we select the appropriate test subjects. Some studios enlist the services of external testing labs. In contrast, others may have an internal testing team that can facilitate the setup and recruitment of user testers based on the game's target demographic. These individuals must be chosen to provide unbiased feedback. Additionally, they should not fall too far outside the range of our target user personas. For instance, testing a violent or scary game on children would not be suitable, while testing a football game on individuals interested in the sport would yield valuable insights.

The old computing phrase "Garbage In, Garbage Out" (GIGO) refers to the concept that poor-quality input produces poor-quality output. The tested item must be accurate and contain all essential elements to support the design intent but doesn't have to reflect the final quality. If the test is to see if exploding barrels are "satisfying," you can't accurately test it without smoke, fire, or sound. Without those elements, the data obtained would be pointless. You need the essential ingredients for an effective test.

By conducting usability testing throughout the development process, designers can check that the systems are working as intended, refine the overall design, and ensure that the game is enjoyable and easy to use for the broader target audience.

Survey

After playtesting the game with users, we need to acquire their feedback. We do so with questionnaires and surveys. Users are not experts in your game, though they may be experts in others. They don't know how something *should work* in your game. We want to dig deep into their feelings, needs, and understandings. Remember, the playtesters are not a focus group defining the game *they* want to make; they are helping improve yours. It's about testing the clarity of what you put out against what you intended.

We start by asking questions based on frustration, favourites, and desires and getting the test users to describe their answers. Are the users completing your game's objectives? Do they understand the plot? We can also ask specifically focused questions.

The following is not a comprehensive list of questions to ask but serves as a framework for creating an effective survey.

Frustration

- *What was the most frustrating moment?*
- *What was the most confusing aspect?*
- *Which part did you find most challenging?*

The answers may not reflect the issues you want or need to fix. They may be valid in the experience you are trying to deliver. You want to ensure the players are not challenged, confused, or frustrated by the **wrong** things.

Favourite

- *What was your favourite moment?*
- *Which aspect was the most enjoyable or memorable?*
- *What made it enjoyable, memorable, or your favourite?*

Find out what they enjoyed and why. The results can go a long way to affirm ideas that don't need to change. Equally, it can shine a light on areas that you hadn't put much faith or energy behind but are connecting with your audience and something you can highlight more as a feature.

Wanted

- *Was there anything you had in mind but could not accomplish?*
- *Is there anything you wish you were able to do?*

Are their needs being met? Are they seeing an opportunity we missed? It could be a terrible idea or something that conflicts with the game's vision—but perhaps not. Ensure they describe why they want or wish to do something.

The Magic Wand

Give your player an imaginary magic wand, and then ask:

- *If you had a magic wand, what would you want to zap away, change, or add?*

Asking them to become wizards might seem strange, but it suggests anything is possible. The player may have insight into what is throwing off the experience and potentially provide the elusive missing ingredient.

Doing

- *What were you doing in the experience?*
- *What objectives did you have?*
- *What actions did you have to take to achieve the goals?*

It's crucial to confirm if your goals for the player were clear. It's less critical that they completed them than that they understood them and knew what they needed to do. These can also be essential follow-up questions for their wants and frustrations.

- *What were you doing at the time?*
- *What did you think you were meant to do at the time?*

Describe

- *How would you describe this game to your friends and family?*
- *How would you describe your overall impression of the game?*

Did their description accurately reflect your vision? Are you happy with the way they talk about the experience? The aims is to see where we are on target, whether our assumptions were correct, and where we must focus more effort. Some studios will focus on the positives of a survey (survivorship or confirmation bias) and ignore the wants and frustrations. Focusing purely on the wins and the things they got "right" means ignoring severe issues. The feedback we don't receive is almost as important as the feedback we do.

However, feedback should be contextualised. Some results can be random misnomers that don't require a reactive approach but rather a reflective one. One player struggling with a feature doesn't mean that feature needs to be torn out, but that perhaps something else was preventing it from being fully understood.

Addressing UX Issues

When encountering UX issues based on user feedback, it's vital to retain a systematic approach to addressing them:

1. Identify and understand the root cause of the issue. *Fall in love with the problem.*
2. Analyse the player data to grasp the various behaviour issues, interactions, and preferences from a heuristic perspective.
3. Once the issue has been identified, evaluate potential solutions conduct a workshop to explore them.
4. Analyse other games in the same genre or category to understand best practices and trends.
5. Collaborate with other team members to gather different perspectives on the issues and help establish ideas.

After evaluating potential solutions, implement the necessary changes. Focus on resolving the problem with minor, manageable fixes rather than introducing one significant drastic change. Simple tweaks introduce fewer variables, making verifying the impact much more manageable. Introducing new problems at this stage can overshadow the original problem.

Additional user testing must be conducted to repeat the conditions of the previous test and assess if the outcome changes. Gather feedback from players and note if other issues are identified. As you continue to develop, monitor the player experience closely. Constantly analyse player behaviour, track engagement and retention metrics, and conduct ongoing usability tests. You can ensure your game remains fresh, exciting, and engaging by making iterative improvements over time.

THE UX REALITY

UX is about removing friction, but games need some friction because it enhances the fun. Walking around an empty environment with no traversal, clues, story, enemies, or changing stakes is not engaging. That's where the friction should come from. There is no fire without friction. This is the realm in which great game UX design shines.

> **"A game with no friction is effectively a screensaver."**
> - Jordan DeVries UI/UX Lead (Jedi Team)

We experience things differently, and we have different external factors outside the game that are often not a choice and cannot be controlled or changed. The extent of that friction and that challenge is relative, and what is challenging for you might not be challenging enough for someone else. Therein lies the need for balance to accommodate different needs.

You may be unable to implement everything the research and data tell you. You will make mistakes and bad calls. Those decisions may be entirely out of your hands. Getting the stakeholders to set aside their own desires and adhere to recommendations can be tricky. The game design is king and will often trump logical findings. Sometimes, searching for alternative ways to excite and shock players is a good thing. Unlike websites and apps, games primarily offer entertainment, fantasy, and escapism, rather than selling a product or a service.

As people age, tastes change. New generations have different memories, values, and understandings of the world. Every game is unique, and UX designers must constantly reassess their approach. Games are a form of creative art, and although a commercial product (some are designed purely to extract money), they are generally not mass-produced commodities with uniform constraints. The introduction of new features, evolving trends, and technological advancements constantly reshapes the gaming landscape.

Making a great game is about *finding the fun*. As I said, UX is not an exact science; it's organic and natural. As much as some people in this discipline will argue, their chosen UX approach often diametrically opposes players' needs, and they'll wonder why it's not working. Humans are not perfect, and you cannot always predict behaviour. UX is primarily about adaptation.

NOTE

1   ablegamers.org/how-the-gaming-industry-is-adapting

UI
"Make it Pretty"

6

FORM *VS* FUNCTION

There have been many moments in my life when I've had to summon all my strength and bite my tongue. I've heard this irritating, chalkboard-scratching phrase 'Make it Pretty' uttered to me and others in this line of work. It's equal parts patronising, diminishing, and reductive. Every fibre of my being wants me to whip my head around and snap with, *"How about you make a less over-encumbered, convoluted, inaccessible mess of a design that no amount of UI will save?"*

Okay, it would be best if you didn't say that to anyone, especially your superiors. (Save this for when you need to vent in your book.) These comments are often said in jest to downplay their own artistic skills. However, a few individuals still use this reductive statement, and it simply infers how much knowledge and respect they have for the craft. Just try to keep your cool. (You could try to ask them politely not to diminish your role and then watch them sweat.) The point I will attempt to make is this: UI is a seamless blend of emotion, design, interaction, brand, and art principles. It's not a *nice* paint-over.

Game UI is a delicate dance between aesthetics and functionality, designed to delight and inspire wonder while avoiding annoyance and confusion.

Like other art forms, games can be beautiful and inspire emotions. They can excite and scare you, encourage social change, and move deeply. Can UI do that, too, or is it limited to characters and the story? How does one attempt to achieve the same emotional resonance from a rectangle and some text? How do you strike a balance that makes very information-heavy games (where they whack every element possible on the HUD) and expect it to look *artistically pleasing?*

DOI: 10.1201/9781003367116-6

Indeed, "looking good" is arguably subjective. However, there are fundamentals we can use to ensure something continues to serve its function while remaining visually appealing. Combining traditional art and fundamental graphic design principles creates excellent UI design. We don't have to make cold and lifeless links between humans and machines. It can be art that is remembered and stands the test of time. It can even be something people cosplay at conventions.

Form follows function is an architecture and industrial design principle from the late 19th and early 20th centuries. It suggests that an object's form should be determined by its intended function, encouraging designers to prioritise an object's practical use and functionality rather than its aesthetic appeal.

However, can form not also be part of the function? In Chapter 4, we discussed how people tend to perceive aesthetic quality to imply better functionality, so I argue that whilst UI is critical in providing information and guidance, visuals create value, too, which adds to the overall function.

It feels like we have become so obsessed with functionality that some UI has become *too* functional. There have been fantastic technical improvements as game engines now embrace UI development. And I love that UX is now generally recognised as a necessity. But I fear that the journey stops at "make this pretty" again in many places. There is a fear of "breaking the UX," so they paint over the same layouts with identical rectangles and text and ship it. It feels that it's becoming increasingly rare to see wireframes being innovated into something beautiful and memorable. Is UI Art dying?

This isn't the case everywhere. I am just saying that if you want all your UI floating around in a fish tank like food scraps because it would suit that game and make it memorable, then why not? There will undoubtedly be challenges, but that sparks innovation and fond memories. If it's possible, why not go for it?

KNOW YOUR PLATFORM

The first step is knowing what platform you'll be designing for. Is it VR (virtual reality), mobile phone, console, or PC? Or all? This information will help you understand the limitations and overall scope. Each platform has its nuances and requirements. Layouts between platforms may differ; trends, technology requirements, and graphical fidelity will vary. Mobile devices have smaller screens, meaning the UI must be adjusted for smaller screens and fingers. PCs can vary in components, displays, performance, and mouse and keyboard. Consoles have stringent platform certification checks and set specifications. VR games require a different approach altogether, as the player is fully immersed in a virtual environment, and specific traditional methods can become uncomfortable to use and look at with the monitor strapped to your face.

Despite their differences, they aim to provide players with a seamless and immersive gaming experience. Therefore, it is vital to understand the platform to ensure the UI approach is suitable and optimised to meet the requirements.

PRINCIPLES OF VISUAL DESIGN

Visual design principles are crucial in creating a functional and visually appealing interface. With the proper application, designers can maintain usability and convey the desired tone of the game to make a lasting impression.

Consistency

UI elements should have a consistent visual language, movement, design, and layout to aid user intuition and look polished.

Hierarchy

Elements must be arranged to create a clear and compelling order of importance. It helps players locate important information or interactive elements on the screen using design techniques such as size, colour, contrast, and placement.

Contrast

Contrast refers to the degree of variance between two or more elements to differentiate them from the rest of the interface. It is a powerful tool for creating visual interest and helping establish hierarchy.

White space

White space (negative space) is the area between elements left blank or unmarked. It can create a sense of balance, contrast, and hierarchy to draw attention to particular aspects. Adequate and intentional use can help declutter the UI and make it easier to navigate.

Typography

Appropriate typography (your font and typeface choices) is used primarily for readability and can help convey the game's desired tone, mood, and voice.

Colour

Colour can convey emotions, style, and contrast. However, not everyone sees colour similarly, so it cannot be the only identifier.

Simplicity

Keep visuals simple when information is heavy to reduce cognitive load.

Balance

Balance refers to how the elements are arranged in a composition to create a sense of equilibrium or stability. There are two types of balance: symmetrical balance, which is achieved when elements are mirrored or repeated along a central axis; and asymmetrical balance, which is achieved through carefully arranging elements of varying sizes and weights to develop an understanding of equilibrium without mirroring.

UI REPRESENTATION

When designing a new UI, it's essential to consider its role within the game and how best players will utilise the information. Instead of simply overlaying all the information on the screen and hoping players will *get it*, consider whether there's a more effective or engaging way to present it.

The types of representation are categorised into four contextual categories: non-diegetic, diegetic, spatial, and meta. Each has its visual pros and cons and unique scheduling and budgeting requirements. The distinction is based on two simple axes: diegesis and spatiality. Classifying these components is not often straightforward, as some UI examples blur the lines.

To best represent your UI, you must first consider the art direction and overall creative vision for the game. Then, you must establish if this UI element is part of the story and if it needs to sit in the scene's space.

Non-Diegetic

Non-diegetic refers to elements outside the context of a game's narrative—things not seen, heard, or interacted with by characters. It's an abstraction that exists purely for the player's benefit. You can choose a style that matches the themes and environments of the game, opt for a contrasting style, or go for a minimalist approach to not overshadow the rest of the frame. A fantasy game may have skeuomorphic features. (Skeuomorphic refers to interfaces that mimic real-world objects and textures.)

A significant advantage of the non-diegetic approach, and why it's most common, is that it's straightforward to design, implement, and implement. It's not effortless, but you don't have to worry about embedding it in the world or placing it on characters. The development is not dependent on different disciplines and the game's moving parts. The main issue with a non-diegetic approach is overuse and overreliance. The player wants to see the game, not the UI. Covering the screen with every possible piece of information can lead to information overload and fatigue from too many stimuli. It doesn't make a bad game better.

Meta

An interface considered "meta" exists in the game's reality, but not in the 3D space. The characters may or may not be aware of it. From subtle hints in your peripheral or quite literally shoved in your face, they can be represented as simple, full-screen overlays, like the POV down a sniper scope or showing changes in health, abilities, and pain as the screen fills with blood. The character is experiencing that pain, but we are seeing it. The driver in the race car sees the fuel and speed gauge on the dashboard, but we, the players, will see a blown-up version on our screens. Meta UI provides information in a way that blends into the narrative for a smooth and immersive gaming experience. It can be very subtle or intrusive when necessary.

Spatial

Spatial UI aims to integrate seamlessly into the game's three-dimensional space. This is beneficial because we can communicate orientation information to the player over three axes. The widgets you see on the field in sports games track which player avatars are passing to and how far a ball may travel. But the digital athletes aren't aware of the widgets, as those exist abstract from the world.

Rocket League (2015) has a three-dimensional arrow in "Ball Cam Mode," pointing out the ball's world position. A circular expanding and contracting graphic flush with the field shows how high the ball is (contracted) and where it will land (expanded). Some games also have the classic arc, depicting the direction, distance, and drop-off curve for weapons such as grenades or arrows.

Spatial UI doesn't just need to be used for gameplay. *Splinter Cell Conviction* (2010) had some incredible typographic tutorials projected onto walls and cover points in three-dimensional space. They were dynamic, retained immersion, and, most importantly, looked fantastic.

This form of UI can make the experience more immersive and provide more precise information in the context of the gameplay. However, these solutions require more resources and art direction to integrate with the game aesthetic.

Diegetic

Diegetic UI is designed to be incorporated into the game world. The character is aware of the interfaces integrated into the narrative. The character could be holding them; they might be connected to their bodies or something they interact with, serving as a conduit for the player. In an FPS game, we might display the player's ammo count on an LED display on the side of their weapon. The player may use a physical treasure map in their hand rather than accessing it via a menu screen. These types of UI are intended to enhance immersion and realism. It can take up less space on the screen and reduce information overload.

In *Dead Space* (2008/2023), the main character has, instead of a health bar, a segmented vibrant pipe that runs up their spine to indicate their health. The post-apocalyptic *Fallout* franchise introduced *The Pip-Boy*, a wearable wrist computer that contains all the in-game menus.

Diegetic UI can be a significant and unique selling point (USP), becoming synonymous with the brand. However, it can present a considerable challenge to developers. The implementation requires many teams working together to ensure it is realistically and effectively woven into the game and still readable and functional. As a result, they are more prone to problems as things change or break. If the environment lighting is broken, the player can no longer see the map in the character's hand. Performance and production costs are significant, so choosing this interface style needs to be carefully considered.

DO I HAVE YOUR ATTENTION?

Each of us has a variable cognitive load and attention span. It's impossible to display everything on the screen simultaneously and expect people to absorb and focus on each element effectively. The director can kick, scream, and slam on tables all they want; *it ain't happening.* When designing the layout and visuals for UI, we must consider why something is displayed to determine when it appears, how it looks, and where it goes.

Attentional Spotlight

If all the world is a stage, your eyes are the spotlight. We focus on what grabs us and on our peripheral vision, which alerts us when a tiger attacks. We cannot assume that players will know where to look, and we must work hard to guide their attention to ensure they do not miss crucial information and avoid failure and frustration. Even in a game where seemingly little is happening, an abundance of information still competes for our attention. We must focus, balance, and place information and feedback in a hierarchy; otherwise, we risk overwhelming the player.

Endogenous and Exogenous Attention

Endogenous and exogenous attention are two distinct types of attention. Endogenous is a conscious, voluntary choice to focus on something, such as reading a book. On the other hand, exogenous is when your attention is involuntary, like when you hear a loud noise and instinctively turn your head to determine the cause.

The player's desires drive endogenous events. If a player wants to find out where to go next, they might open their quest menu to search for a location.

For this scenario, we want to ensure consistency in objective phrasing, iconography, and presentation between the map and the navigation system in the HUD. Searching your Settings menu doesn't have every option screaming out at you for attention; they are balanced. We highlight the one you are currently hovering over so you know where you are.

Exogenous events in a game occur unexpectedly and are not something the player intentionally seeks out. Such events may include incoming attacks, accidentally unplugging the controller, or receiving a message from another player. When trying to gain or direct the players' attention to these events, it's crucial to consider the impact of the players' central gameplay area view. Appearing in the peripheral might avoid impacting the primary gameplay area, but it is easy to ignore. It might be an element that is okay to ignore based on its hierarchy of importance. It may be critical to warn the player directly in the middle of the screen, but we don't want to block their gameplay, so they can't do anything about it. Sometimes, we have to do this if it's imperative.

Useful Field of View (UFOV)

The useful field of view is the screen area where players shine the "spotlight" in a game. The proportion of that area can vary in each game, as does how much visual information can be presented and understood at a glance. This bearing is vital as it helps designers balance layouts to prioritise information that requires quick reactions, compared to those that are safe to ignore till later. It's also not wise to assume that related information can be placed on opposing sides of the screen. A person's age can also determine their UFOV. Developing children have constricted views, and as we age or if our sight is impaired, our UFOV decreases. A smaller UFOV can limit our awareness and cause us to miss critical information, leading to mistakes. We must consider our target demographic carefully when defining our layouts to ensure we allow for the best visual awareness and processing ability.

Inattentional Blindness

Inattentional blindness occurs when a person fails to notice an unexpected object or event in their visual field, even when it's right in front of them. This happens because our brains have a limited capacity for attention. We can only focus on a small portion of our visual field at any given time, and different events and varying stimuli fight for our limited attention. The player may overlook key details if the UI is cluttered with distracting visual elements. It's crucial to remove obstacles hindering their attentional spotlight.

Game designers often complain when players don't understand their carefully thought-out game mechanics. They believe they have made them *very* clear and concise. Unfortunately, instead of thoroughly reviewing the core issues, it often leads to "doubling down" on adding more UI to fix the problem (*fix it in UI*). However, the real issue is that players' attention is frequently drawn to competing things. The mechanic might be fine, but it's not receiving focus, and designers need to consider the attentional spotlight.

UI Channels

UI channels refer to how information is presented to the player. Effective use is crucial for guiding players' attention and enhancing their overall experience. Visual channels are the primary route, but auditory cues, tactile feedback, and other sensory inputs are often used.

Audial feedback is primarily used to reinforce actions, confirmation, and errors. It's crucial to make attention-grabbing elements more accessible, especially for sightless and visually impaired players. Sound also provides an additional sense of space and direction as it can be placed in three-dimensional space, helping players locate the origin as they would in real life. Players can track down loot chests in hidden areas, be aware of monsters they want to avoid, or listen out for the footsteps of the opposing team. Sound prompts, hints, and effects can help increase engagement and retention. These sounds can help us feel more successful and accomplished in our actions as well as improve immersion.

Haptics (controller or phone vibration) can also create a more engaging and immersive experience. It can grant players a greater tactile sense of their actions or heighten events such as pushing a heavy rock, pressing buttons, or successfully reloading a gun. It provides an accessible route for players with visual and hearing impairments. However, there needs to be a way for players to reduce or deactivate vibrations if they suffer from any motor impairments (e.g., arthritis, muscular dystrophy, carpal tunnel), as this can cause additional stress and pain.

UNDERSTANDING INTERFACES

The interfaces may vary based on the platform, requiring different input layouts. Not all games need a specific HUD feature or screens. The following won't be an exhaustive list of every UI, just the most common, especially regarding HUD, which is built for specific gameplay. For instance, you don't need health bars if your game has no health mechanic or ammo counter if your game is gun-free.

Start Screen

These infamous words, "Press Start, Begin Player One, Insert Coin, or Press Any Button," have been seen on countless pieces of merchandise and used in popular culture as a totem to the video game world. Walk into any arcade, and you will see unoccupied games displaying a game's demo in action. It was a simple and genius way to entice players, and once a coin was inserted, they were prompted to press a start button, which would then grant them access and, in the process, designate a controller. One of the technical reasons we still employ this screen is to check for an input device and assign a controller. In more modern times, the game would establish an Internet connection, link to a server, load the user's profile account, and do other work behind the scenes.

The start screen is the first thing players see, and it sets the initial tone for the entire experience. It typically includes the game's logo, title, and relevant options. The design should be visually attractive and immersive while providing clear and concise information. In more romantic terms, it's a doorway to another world, and pressing that button unlocks the door. It sets the expectation of the incoming reality—anticipation, excitement, and intrigue. If the first five minutes of a game are important, then this first second is critical. A good horror game sends chills down a player's spine on the start screen alone. Setting the tone and DNA of a game in the player's mind via a single screen with limited interaction can be a powerful tool.

Frontend Menus

A game may drop you directly into the action, while others may take you to the main menus first before gameplay begins. These are typically the first point of interaction between the player and the game and serve as a gateway to various game modes, settings, and speciality menus. These menus must be easy to use and have excellent navigation, but we also want them to look cool, evoke the brand, and maintain that excitement established so far. They have a unique style, consistent button language, and attractive animations.

Your main menu will give the player all the primary navigation points to explore. Often, in story-focused (usually single-player) experiences, the ability to continue where you left off is often essential. Some require you to navigate secondary screens to select game modes, connect to online servers and public lobbies, load saves, adjust challenge levels, manage live service features, and access profile and settings screens. The secondary screens broken down further into multiple tertiary screens focusing on display settings, graphics, audio, gameplay, language, controls, and accessibility. A good rule of thumb to keep in mind is that it's okay to have as many screens as required if the flow is in one direction, but if the player needs to navigate backwards, keep your menus two or three levels deep.

Frontend menus are easy to skip, and it's easy to assume a game only starts after the first chapter loads. There's little reason to hang around when a menu only has a few buttons. However, the main menu presents a unique opportunity to start foreshadowing events. This is a chance for players to get in the mood, imagine future encounters, set the scene, and learn mechanics and game loops.

The remastered *BioShock's* (2017) main menu gave the player a clearer glimpse into the world they were about to enter—a crashed plane next to a solitary lighthouse. The three-dimensional *Half-Life 2* (2004) menu backgrounds would change based on how far you were through the game. This would help players remember where they last left off. Some main menus allow you to practise the game's basic mechanics, while others demonstrate a typical game loop. *Left 4 Dead* (2008) started with what most would assume was just a trailer, but the design of what it showed was essentially a flashy but informative tutorial video.

A popular trend in the late 2000s was to use freeze frames from an exciting action sequence as the background for each menu screen. Each navigation change would swoop the camera through the scene till it stops on another exciting composition. *Tom Clancy's Splinter Cell Conviction* (2010) depicted a brutal shootout between agents and gang members. The Settings menu shows one of the unfortunate baddies collapsing painfully onto a bloody banquet table as you adjust audio and picture options. As cool as this may be, also it can also slow down the speed between menu changes, which can be frustrating and is one of the reasons why the trend is less prolific now. Considering what you put behind a menu is crucial, as it can quickly overwhelm the frame.

Settings/Options

Accessibility needs. TVs, sound systems, environments, skills, and personal needs differ. These menus allow players to customise various exposed parameters to better suit their preferences beyond the defaults imposed by the developers. They allow graphical, audio, input, control bindings, UI, language, and specific gameplay elements, allowing players to fine-tune their experience and optimise performance.

Unlike typical menus, these screens can encompass many different widgets with suitable controls based on the setting they are linked to. Some options include a slider so the player can pick any number between a minimum and maximum value. Other options can be to toggle between two values (e.g. on or off) or to choose between incremental set values (low, medium, high).

Heads-up Display (HUD)

A heads-up display, or HUD, is any transparent display of information and data which allows the player not to divert their gaze from the viewport. It originated from military aircraft, where the term "heads up" refers to pilots' being able to continue looking forward rather than down at other instruments and controls. (Which is quite critical when travelling at high speed). In games, players can continue to view the game world whilst being presented with passive and active information, such as vitals, resources, mini-maps, and objective markers, without taking their eyes off the action.

Generally, we attempt to design an unobtrusive HUD that does not interfere with the player's immersion unless necessary or for dramatic effect. The amount of HUD shown depends on the player's needs and the gameplay requirements. Some games often show too much HUD at once, which can cause clutter and cognitive overload, so opting for dynamic reveals and a conservative approach as much as possible is essential.

A well-designed HUD provides players with the information they need to make informed decisions during gameplay, preferably when required. For example, the health bar lets players know how much damage their character can take before they die. The ammo counter lets the player know how many bullets are left before reloading. The mini-map shows an abstract view of the game world and helps navigation. Players will receive visual feedback upon completing a quest, levelling up, or a friend inviting them to join a game, all the while still being able to see the viewport and continue playing. Some of these will offer buttons that take the player out of the game to view a menu or perform an interaction if they want to.

Different games require different HUDs. The HUD design depends on the game's immersion and abstraction level. For example, the HUD might be minimal or non-existent in emotional and cinematic story games. On the other hand, competitive first-person shooters require a strict and concise HUD that doesn't obstruct the view. Real-time strategy (RTS), massive multiplayer games (MMO), and city building games, however, might need to display a lot of information, including tools, drop-down menus, and statistics. While this may seem like a lot of information, it's what many players of these games want.

The HUD is a vital component of a game's UI, providing players with the information they need to make strategic decisions. Developers must carefully consider the design and placement of the HUD to ensure that it is suitable for the genre, practical to the player's needs, and unobtrusive. It's there to enhance gameplay, not hinder it.

In-game Overlays

An in-game overlay displays information on top of gameplay. That might sound vague or like a HUD, but unlike a HUD, the focus is taken away from the gameplay locomotion and instead concentrated on whatever function the overlay provides. Depending on the function, it can pause the action, slow down time, or require the player to perform the activity while exposed to the world. The element overlaps the game graphics and can display information such as menus, maps, inventories, and objectives. The overlay can be designed to be transparent or opaque, taking up the entire screen or only a portion. It must be designed to be easy to read and understand while blending in with the game's graphics and not drastically breaking immersion.

FIND YOUR ROUTE

So now we know what things we can make and how to present them. We need to figure out how things will look. Unless you are responsible for UI art direction, you will probably be working with an art, game, or creative director who will confirm what they are after. Regardless, like planning a long journey, it's worth exploring alternative paths and working with key stakeholders before deciding on the best direction, in this case, establishing your routes.

Routes are essential to figure out before you jump straight into creating interfaces because you want to figure out the best style for the game. Establishing a route also gives you a foundation to always fall back on when you need to make creative decisions or need help. A route summarises your main themes, tonal pillars, and executions.

Depending on the game's theme, its relationship to intellectual property (IP), and the audience, there might be a few clear options; sometimes, the sky is the limit. All routes can lead to the same destination but have different flavours. For example, in a sci-fi game, one route could be very industrial, another high-tech, and yet another one could be organic and alien. All of these may be perfectly viable, and to figure out which one suits best (and satisfies those who might be signing off on it), spending a little time exploring each one may yield dividends.

I usually present three to four routes to a client or director (or myself). I keep the number small to concentrate my ideas and make the process more manageable. Equally, presenting these routes keeps the conversation simple and allows clients or directors to choose (which makes them feel good). Too many options will result in weaker or similar ideas (potentially ones you don't even like) being chosen. Ideally, you want to present options you would be happy to work with and show to your directors that you have a clear idea of how to execute them.

Creating a Route

Through research and creativity, we will fill out a simple template to define each route.

1. **Name**

    It may sound silly, but once you have figured out a possible route, it helps to give it a catchy name. It's a fun way to help define the core concept—a "brand" to use when presenting it to key stakeholders or the team. A name is helpful as it doesn't require you to redescribe the theme whenever it's referred to. It helps to distinguish it from the other routes and can generate excitement in people. For example, you could call a route *retro-futurism, sci-fi prehistoric tribal,* or *space propaganda.*

2. **Slogan**

    Describe your route in one catchy sentence to create intrigue and summarise your proposal to busy directors. For the *sci-fi prehistoric tribal* route, we could say, *"Advanced technology created by an ancient culture using natural resources."*

3. **Pillars**

    The pillars are the fundamental aesthetic aspects that support the visual design. Constraints make the research and creative process more focused.

    Tribal, High-Tech, Mystical, Organic

4. **Execution**

    How do you propose to achieve this? What techniques can you deploy to evoke those feelings? Use words that describe the methods you would use to create this route. Include a few key research images to support your direction.

Glowing Mystical Runes & Symbols / Tribal Patterns / Organic Movement / Natural Materials / Vibrant Colours / Advanced Technology

Genre, Immersion, and Aesthetics

Now that we know how to format our ideas, we must develop some examples. At the start of a project, this can be a daunting task. If it's a brand new IP, this can be even more of a challenge as you have no established conventions on which to base the style, as there are no comics, movies, or previous games to reference.

Firstly, we must consider the UI's role in your game's aesthetic. What kind of game is it? Who is the audience? What are the themes? Is it a new IP or a game for an existing franchise? Don't start collecting references or creating concepts until you have answers.

Even in the early days when the game is still being figured out, we can still plot ourselves on a chart between an immersive experience and an abstract experience. Great UI art immerses us, tells a story, builds a world, expends disbelief, and keeps us informed. We become engrossed in the situation, living that fantasy. Abstraction is recognising that *I am playing a video game*. Where between these two points does this game exist?

To figure out the game's vibe at an early stage, we can look to a few places. We can talk with the directors and understand more about their overall vision. Speak to the writers to find out what the story is all about. Discuss proposed game mechanics with the designers and determine what the player will do throughout the game, what sort of camera they will view the world with, and how they will progress through the story. Additionally, we can review early concept art of the characters and environments. We've already established that the different types of UI representation come at various costs. Diegetic, highly immersive solutions require allocating lots of time and resources. If we plan too late, we must settle for an abstraction, usually a non-diegetic solution that sits over the game's graphics. This may be a game where abstraction is more suitable. For an immersive experience, we can look at the concepts and technology defined in the game world itself. If it's a steampunk game, perhaps the UI art will be based on that. We develop rules off that theme to remain immersive. However, with abstraction, the UI can be a metaphor and can be literally anything that suits the product.

It's helpful to figure out when your game is set. For an immersive experience, we can consider the period, history, anthropology, art, typography, and graphic design of the time or the game's world. For a more abstract direction, we can look at the time we live in now. What will be trending when the game comes out? Has a style of UI or typography come back into fashion?

We need to consider the game's genre. Genre refers to artistic work with common characteristics or themes. In games, genre doesn't just refer to themes like horror or fantasy but also to the game type, such as action, adventure, puzzle, or role-playing. The genre can dictate the best representations based on typical competitive analysis. It's important because it establishes known affordances from which we can draw inspiration. Our competition can show us what audiences expect or are growing tired of.

This entire process is vital to establishing our routes for several reasons. First, we need an idea of what we are working towards and the expected results. Second, we need talking points—areas of discussion and discovery. Once established, the direction becomes the platform for all our future decision-making; all our art and design challenges can be weighed against it.

Research

Shockingly, art direction is not just making *Pinterest* boards. The Internet is a great place to find the latest trends, but it shouldn't be the sole destination to source your references. Art direction is about discovery. Looking beyond the search bar to expand your ideas would be best. Remember, don't stress about trying to be new and innovative, as you will not necessarily invent something new. Often, in art, we are simply mixing styles or being influenced. Frequently, we expand upon ideas of what people have come to know and flip or elevate them. Sometimes, it's a *lighting-in-a-bottle* moment.

I was working on a project set in New York City, and it just so happened that I was going there on vacation during pre-production. I was amazed at the wealth of details you wouldn't find in a Google search. Every subway decal, sewer cover, and art-deco border fell victim to my camera. Raw references that would influence my patterns and shapes that even born and bred New Yorkers wouldn't notice were going in the game. I wasn't creating a new pattern from pure imagination but referencing it from an original source, helping the game look authentic but unique. I'm not expecting anyone to jump on a plane, at a great expense, before each new project. This was just a lucky circumstance. The point is that you've got to get out there. If you rely only on the Internet for your references, you will repeat what has come before.

Some projects aren't set in real locations or at this point in time. If the game is set during a particular historical moment, get to a museum at least. For one project, I had an authentic pair of WW2 binoculars and a sniper scope sitting on my desk. On another, we based our animations on the studio's broken fluorescent lights. We had to get creative with our references and make our own for one project themed around water. I mounted a camera above a leaking fish tank (sat on castor wheels), with a tablet below the water and glass. The tablet displayed some placeholder UI, and simply shaking the wheels simulated the effect of water refraction and realistic caustics on a digital source to use as a reference.

There are plenty of other sources out there. Watch movies in the same genre. Make a playlist of songs you associate with the theme. You can research books from specific periods or subjects, as most of that content cannot be found online. You can even look to nature for new patterns. You don't need to spend a fortune (or any money for that matter), just a little extra effort, to source fresh references that lead to fresh results.

Researching is fun, as this is the moment to explore and discover. However, I recommend maintaining a few housekeeping practices, as it can become unmanageable without these limitations. You can waste time researching things that are not relevant. It's better to have a few strong 'hero' references rather than thousands that detract or are similar. Highlighting key ideas and things you want to avoid is crucial. Research and source images, textures, colour palettes, and typography that capture the mood and tone of the game.

When researching, it's essential to organise and maintain a system. Organise by media type, specific pillars, moods, styles, and themes. Break up your references into subfolders, not just one big 'ideas' folder. Don't forget to make notes about the references you're using. It helps you remember why a reference is useful and what you like or don't like about it.

Collaborate as a team, use rules and tools to stay on track, communicate if someone strays from the core point, and lead by example. When displaying multimedia, you can use software designed for collaborative annotation. Consider planning group trips to the library, exhibitions, or museums.

Practise restraint. Find the best reference and discard the rest. If you're worried about needing it later, put it in a separate folder. Seek out advice from others. If you know someone knowledgeable about history, ask them for recommendations on the best books for a specific subject. They might even lend you some books. Don't dismiss outside opinions and suggestions; you might discover a hidden gem you hadn't considered.

Mood Boards

A mood board is essential when establishing your core ideas and pitching a route. It's a way of visually communicating your thoughts without making anything. It can help to visualise and understand a unified vision. Organise by pillars and keep the choice of reference concentrated. An art or creative director may not have the time or patience to review hundreds of references and then "get" what you are driving at. If you can't summarise your route with a few references, you must step back and continue researching. Keeping the mood board focused and not overwhelming is essential. We want to use this as a tool and reference throughout the design process to ensure consistency.

Style Guides

A style guide is a document that outlines a UI's core visual and design elements. It provides guidelines on using colour, typography, icons, and other elements consistent with the game's brand or theme. It is an essential tool for developers to maintain consistency and unity throughout the development process. Furthermore, it's about communication. This document can spread the message of what the game's UI is about with other departments and new team members, outsourcing and co-dev, and as a general pitch device to directors.

The purpose of a style guide isn't to solve every problem. It provides the tools for artists and designers to face any new challenges. When artists encounter something that hasn't been explicitly covered in the guide, they will have the resources to tackle it.

In its simplest form, a style guide boils down to *this, not this*. It lays out the rules of engagement, the tactics for achieving the visual goal, and the boundaries and platform for where to explore. Great ideas can't grow without it, but we must ensure consistency; otherwise, we lose unity entirely. Showing examples of how things need to be used and how they shouldn't helps define the goalposts. A big tick or cross goes a long way in ensuring clarity.

Mockups and Previs

A UI pre-vis (pre-visualisation), high-fidelity mockup, or prototype is a detailed and polished visual representation of the game's final UI form. It is typically created using design software such as Adobe Photoshop, XD, After Effects, Sketch, or Figma (or whatever you want). These tools are used to help visualise and test the UI before implementation. It provides an opportunity to experiment with the best solutions. This process can also help identify potential problems or conflicts early on, saving time and resources. The mockup includes all UI elements, such as menus, buttons, icons, and text, and is designed to be as close to the final product as possible.

The Rule of Cool

Games can be fun, artistic, and immersive experiences, so there is some lee-way to sacrifice what would be *technically* a better UX for something that looks cool. *The Rule of Cool* is a design principle prioritising visual appeal and aesthetic value over practicality or realism. It suggests that certain elements can be included in a work simply because they look subjectively "cool," amusing, or visually striking to enhance the overall experience.

However, it can also be a controversial principle, as some argue that it can lead to impractical or nonsensical designs that detract from the function. This isn't an excuse to shut out your UX designer (if it's not you). Talk to and involve them with your intentions and see if they can help. We all want to make a great experience, but making something cool can also be the goal. Yes, this menu works great, feels responsive, and does everything it needs to do, but it's a dull, forgettable experience. Could making it more exciting lead to a better UX? Could it be cooler?

UI
Survival Guide

7

UI SYSTEMS

UX isn't a linear process. There is a lot of back-and-forth. Sometimes, things 'look good on paper' and work well in prototypes, but they can no longer feel right with time, exposure, iteration, and, most importantly, after adding the art. This dynamic nature of UI/UX design is not a flaw but a feature. It allows for adaptability and iteration, ensuring the final product meets players' ever-evolving needs.

Possessing a broad knowledge of variable design patterns and systems to enhance or fix challenges is highly beneficial. There is nothing wrong with deciding something that isn't working and switching to something better suited. Challenge brings discomfort and rewards. This is how you *survive*.

UI systems are a collection of reusable UI components and design patterns. These systems cover various aspects, such as input routing, navigation, and menu management. Using a UI system is not just a choice but a strategic decision. It ensures visual design and functionality consistency. It also promotes efficiency by allowing designers to reuse existing components, saving time and effort. Additionally, a UI system facilitates scalability, making it easier to add new features and functionality easier. Lastly, it encourages collaboration among designers, developers, and stakeholders by providing a shared language.

Menu Manager

A menu manager oversees the various menus the player interacts with. It is responsible for creating, displaying, and controlling the flow of menus and is

DOI: 10.1201/9781003367116- 7

designed to provide consistent and intuitive interactions. It also allows game developers to add new menu options or modify existing ones without having to change the underlying code.

Focus System

Focus refers to the state of the currently selected or otherwise active UI component. A UI component is "focused" when it is available to receive an input, such as a button pressed on the gamepad, a finger on the screen, or a mouse click. It's a simple but crucial UI technique that ensures the user knows where they are and where their input will be directed.

Input Handling and Management

Input handling is receiving and responding to user input, such as mouse clicks, keyboard presses, or touch gestures, to trigger specific actions or events within the UI. The UI recognises the user's actions and provides them with the expected feedback or outcome. It's crucial for complex and multilayered menus. Input routing handles the navigation to the appropriate data assets, functions, or actions in a game. It ensures that when users click or interact with a specific part of the interface, their input is detected and directed to the right thing.

Input Methods and Navigation

What input method is suitable for your project depends on the technology, platform, and type of game. With touch-based input, your thumb and fingers are the primary input sources for tablet and phone products. The amount of pressure, direction, and motion detected in a designated area routes the input to the assigned function. This requires developers to consider how much space the screen needs for effective input detection. Designers must also consider the operator's physical characteristics, limitations, structure, strength, and mobility. Some mobile games are designed to be played with one hand or in landscape mode, requiring both hands, like a portable handheld game device. If you put small buttons in difficult-to-reach places and use complex gestures, your touchscreen game will not be an enjoyable experience.

   With the advent of home consoles, handheld gamepads quickly replaced the joystick and paddle controllers, allowing players to interact with games more intuitively. Over the years, gamepads have evolved and undergone various design changes, leading to the advanced ergonomic controllers we have today. The interaction design of a game that utilises a controller is reasonably straightforward due to its natural limitations. By that, you only have so many buttons and combinations (button combos) to work with. Unlike designing for mobile phones, we don't have to worry about ergonomics as much. As controllers advanced, so did the interaction and input designs, leading to excellent access to more options as we navigated menus and gameplay. However, this brings more challenges as the systems grow more complex and we run out of buttons or make input too complicated.

Navigating a menu with just a D-pad was simple. When analog sticks were used for navigation, players had greater control but had to adapt to thumb agility and stick design. "Free Cursor" navigation, popularised by *Destiny* (2014), offers more flexibility but can be less accessible and requires more engineering resources to execute correctly. It's excellent for specific scenarios (like grid layouts), but can be cumbersome and annoying if implemented poorly.

When building a game for PC, ensure the mouse and keyboard can operate your interactions—not one or the other, but both. You should be able to click buttons with a mouse, navigate to them with keys, or press a single key to activate them. Use WASD *and* arrow keys for directional navigation. It would help if you also considered designing interactions for left-handed PC players.

VR probably needs its own book because traditional doesn't work here. Players interact inside a world, so the UI has to be spatial or diegetic. We opted for natural affordances in *Batman: Arkham VR* (2016), meaning Batman used big tactile buttons and a Bat... *iPad?* Designing tablet interactions inside VR was pretty weird, but you don't have to explain it. Some consistent trends are formed in the VR space, but it's still open waters, so you can explore with an open mind.

DESIGN PATTERNS

The naming and classification of widgets and design patterns can be contentious. Some labels emerged from the physical world, some are legacies, and some have emerged from popular trends and coffee shops. Do not worry too much about it. There is a bunch of gatekeeping around it, but you shouldn't care; players don't, and the name is unimportant. What is essential is the function.

A design pattern is a reusable solution to a common problem. These patterns can include menus, input forms, and buttons, which can be customised to suit specific needs. Designers can use patterns as guidelines to save time and effort and ensure consistency and familiarity.

There is no one-size-fits-all or standard approach when building a menu system or HUD. We pick what suits the needs of the game and the players. Indeed, trends, markets, and functional necessities can often dictate standards. However, in UX and UI, we choose the best tool for the task, not just the best tool we have.

The following will not be an exhaustive list of every UI element *ever*. I've attempted to amalgamate the most common and focus on professional, technical terminology.

Text

Text, text fields, and text boxes house the written content on the UI. This includes everything from button labels to in-game dialogue, conversation choices, tutorials, hints, controller callouts, scores, and objectives. Designers can control justification, style, and font selection. Some text is pre-written; others originate from real-time actions, such as your score, damage, or combo numbers.

The text that comes with the game is called "strings." A text string refers to an ID referencing an assigned text. So when you see the *"You Died"* plastered over your screen when you are fatally unsuccessful in a game, that is a string. Each ID contains variations of the same line for each language the game ships in. Localisation teams (who adapt the game text for each language) prepare translations for each ID, so when the UI detects a language change, the ID switches to the corresponding column rather than a new string.

When designing, it's imperative to consider how strings expand. Most strings are variable and can change based on many factors, such as language, where translations can double or triple, and character length. Even different level names, player names, and subtitles can vary in length but occupy the same text field. We must provide enough vertical or horizontal room for them to expand or adjust dynamically. Otherwise, we must take drastic measures.

- **Scale to fit:** The area expands based on the data it receives.
- **Text-scaling:** The font increases or decreases in size based on the fixed area defined for it.
- **Truncation:** It is an uncommon drastic measure in which the text field can add an ellipse (...).

- **Scrolling Text:** This is a 'blunt object' solution. If a text string becomes too long for a fixed field, the contents will automatically start to animate to reveal the hidden text and continue to loop.
- **Scroll Boxes:** The text can sometimes become multiple paragraphs. If the space available is at its maximum, a scroll box allows the player to manually move the text in and out of view by using a scroll bar.

Well-designed text should be concise and easily read, with appropriate font sizes, colours, and styles. It's critical to consider your audience's reading level, the game's tone, and accessibility when writing text. This isn't a case of "dumbing things down," but just making sure our text isn't convoluted and unnecessarily lengthy. If you can say the same thing in fewer words, then do that. If adding an extra word or two adds value, like a comedic tone, or helps add to the fantasy, that's fine, too, if the design intent is still evident. For example, in *Helldivers 2* (2024), when the game is loading, it says, *"Please wait democratically."*

Images

A picture is indeed worth a thousand words. Images can anchor a layout with an essential piece of visual detail. Iconography often conveys more information across borders, between cultures, and among people than any text usually can. Images don't need to be translated, though some territories have cultural and legal constraints. Every image encapsulates all the themes and pillars of the brand, no matter how inconsequential it appears. Images can also refer to simple things, like solids, gradients, button backgrounds, shapes, and dividing lines.

Buttons

If you had to summarise the UI as one widget, the humble button would be it. It is a single asset that will be used countless times. Buttons can direct players to new locations and unlock hidden treasures. You must ensure that three significant factors are covered in your buttons. They need to be **familiar** (consistent and noticeable as an interactive element), **accessible** (it doesn't rely on only one channel of feedback), and have a **clear visual hierarchy** (contrast in visuals and information).

The anatomy of a button comprises a few essential components. Firstly, we need a text label or icon to know what the button does or where it goes. The button needs some indication of its interactive space—where the cursor

or finger needs to hit. When using text, we must consider how it might scale and expand the button and not look strange when stacked with other buttons.

Buttons also need various display conditions to react to input. The amount of conditions required depends on the platform the game is on. Each state change needs different visual cues, such as colour, size, movement, and shape, to communicate the button's state to the player.

These states can include:

Default state: The button's standard state before any interaction.
Hover state or **focused state:** The button appears ready to receive input when in focus.
Pressed state: When the player initiates input.
Deactivated state: When deactivated, it may appear locked or greyed out to indicate it's not currently accessible.
Selected state: A button may have a selected state indicating that it is active or chosen.

Progress Bars

The progress bar is a graphical representation of the minimum and maximum values between which a value can float. They can be visually represented in several ways, such as the traditional left-to-right horizontal bars, radial bars,

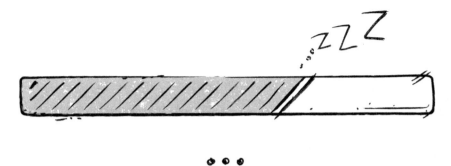

segmented circles, vertical bars that fill from the bottom to the top, or even a fraction of a circle. This is helpful for things like a racing game's speedometer, making a basic progress bar look more exciting or integrating it into a mini-map.

When the player loads a level, uses a resource, or progresses towards a goal, the length or size of the graphic "fill" inside the bounds (a secondary graphic representing the minimum and maximum values) changes based on the context. It empties to zero to imply the player has less of something as they use or lose it (like power or health), or fills to show regain, time, or progress. They can represent static values, like weapons or character stats. Progress bars can help players stay motivated by providing a sense of accomplishment and an indication of progress so they don't grow bored waiting for something.

Menus

A menu is a collection of options or commands. This essential component provides players with a convenient way to interact with the game and access its features. Typically, frontend-driven options are equally utilised in gameplay, allowing access to game settings, inventory, and weapon upgrades. The menu choice is generally defined by its contents and the input method. There are some common trends and technical constraints, but, typically, it depends on the player's needs and what works best for that game.

Accordion Menu

An accordion menu allows players to navigate hierarchical content by expanding and collapsing menu sections within a group of buttons. They save space by allowing users to view only the relevant information. Additionally, accordion menus facilitate easy navigation through a large amount of content.

However, a large amount of content can lead to clutter and confusion, and players may not be aware of the collapsed content. Some players may find the interaction with the accordion menu confusing, as it's unclear which sections are expandable and collapsible. They may not be accessible to players who use screen readers, as the structure may not be conveyed accurately.

Drop-down Menu

A list of options appears when a player clicks, presses, or hovers over a drop-down menu. Grouping related options can save space and simplify navigation. However, it can restrict visibility and make accessing specific options cumbersome on certain platforms.

Radial Menu

A radial menu is a circular menu with options around a central point. When the player interacts with the menu, the options rotate around a central point,

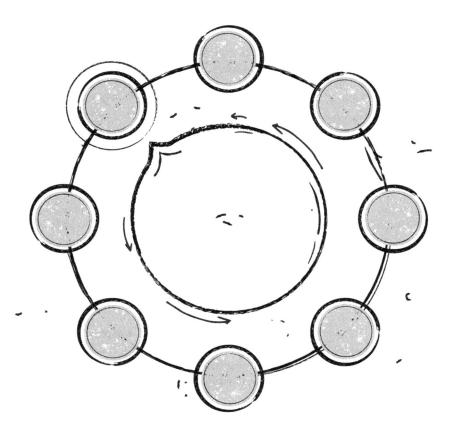

with the selected option appearing at the top of the circle, or a graphic indicator representing the inputs rotates to highlight each option. Radial menus' circular shape makes them more intuitive and easy for players to use. However, due to their shape, they are limited in the number of options they can accommodate. Beyond a specific number, using a radial menu can become cumbersome and challenging.

Hamburger Menu

A hamburger menu (technically known as a slide drawer icon or navigation) is commonly used in mobile applications and websites. When pressed, it reveals a list of the user's options or actions. Hamburger menus save screen space, making them particularly suitable for mobile devices and familiar to many users, which can enhance navigation. However, their hidden nature may pose discoverability and accessibility challenges. It's important to note that despite the name, they are not actually edible!

Grid Menu

A grid menu displays its options in a grid-like pattern. The grid can be uniform or asymmetrical, showing a hirearchy of importance (more essential items getting a larger grid element size) or just making an exciting layout. They are popular due to their clear organisation and visual appeal. Grid menus are most suitable for displaying a limited number of options. They can be made scrollable to navigate a vast grid, which can be challenging and overwhelming, especially on a gamepad.

Flyouts

A flyout menu appears when the user hovers over a specific element. The menu "flies out" and displays options or actions. Unlike dropdown menus, the source of a flyout can be in any location in a broad enough area. Flyout menus offer a clean UI but pose discoverability and accessibility challenges.

Tab Menu

A tab menu displays options in separate tabs or panels the player can switch between (reminiscent of old suspended folders with tabs in a filing cabinet). With each switch, screens or a collection of further options appears within the same shell menu. This menu is common in most console games due to its speed of use, especially with the introduction of the trigger and shoulder buttons. It reduces the number of menu layers as the player stays on the same screen, but the contents change. Tabs are helpful for categories but are limited by horizontal screen space, so they work best when only displaying a few options.

Cross Menu

A cross menu displays actions around a central point, often arranged in a cross shape. The shape is frequently inspired by how the player usually navigates it with the direction pad. Cross menus, commonly found in HUDs, offer simplicity and organisation by representing options with icons. Due to their innate shape and interaction input, they are best suited to limited options, as they can take up significant space and become cumbersome to navigate.

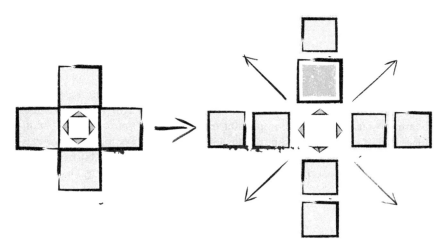

Cards

Cards are commonly used to display information in a visually appealing and organised way. They are usually rectangular and typically group related information like a traditional playing card. They often contain a summary, an image, or an icon for quick identification, leveraging our familiarity with real-life cards. Cards can be easily resized and rearranged, making them ideal for responsive design. Another benefit is that they take advantage of *the principle of common region.* Multiple items contained within a boundary are more likely to be viewed as being in the same group.

However, if too many cards are displayed on the screen simultaneously, it can be overwhelming. Additionally, if the card information is too complex, it may not fit within the limited space on the screen or the player's cognitive capacity. Ensure a good hierarchy level with your labels, details, and images. Be cohesive and consistent with the layout and strive for simplicity. Finally, provide enough white space to allow elements inside the card to breathe.

Loader / Throbber / Progress

A loader or throbber is a micro animation that appears on the screen while the game is loading or waiting for a specific action to complete. According to the Doherty threshold principle, we need something to keep the player's attention, or they will assume the product is unusable.

Modal

A modal overlay (sometimes called a "pop-up") is an element that appears on top of the main game screen and requires the player to interact. It is commonly used to present important information or options, such as confirmation or error prevention. By design, modal overlays force an interruption, impacting the player's immersion, so they should be used infrequently. They can also cause frustration if the instruction is confusing or difficult to close.

Notifications

Notifications keep the player informed about essential occurrences and keep them on track with objectives. They appear on the screen as small messages after completing a particular action or triggering an event, for example, you have collected something new, finished a task, completed an achievement, or a friend is asking to join your game. Unlike a modal, notifications will remain for a limited time and won't pause gameplay or take over the screen. They are generally passive and do not require input, but they can give input options that route the player elsewhere. If designed poorly or used excessively, it can become distracting and annoying.

Sliders and Steppers

Sliders and steppers allow players to adjust numerical values with a graphical widget. A slider changes a value by *sliding* a handle along a horizontal or vertical track, while a stepper enables the player to increase or decrease a value by *steps*. These elements are intuitive by nature, allowing players to quickly understand their purpose and operation. They also provide a visual representation of the current value. They can also pose challenges regarding their accuracy and may not provide the granularity required for specific values.

Separators and Spacers

Separators are visual elements used to divide sections of the UI. They can be horizontal or vertical lines or other minimal graphic elements. They provide space between elements so that players can perceive groups and separation. Spacers offer the same deal but utilise blank space instead of a graphical element.

Carousel

A carousel (like the fairground ride) displays a single image or label from a set, one at a time. The player can navigate the content independently or loop automatically. This is great for saving screen space and focusing choices. It's good to show how many options are in a carousel by featuring a graphical indicator below the current choice (and where that choice is in that indicator). If they contain too many options, it can be cumbersome to use.

Checkboxes and Toggle Switches

Checkboxes represent a clear boolean choice (a data type with only two possible values: true or false, zero or one). They are one of the earliest graphical UI elements. They are usually represented by a square box that can be checked or unchecked.

The toggle is another binary control that switches between two states and indicates the current state. It benefits from being reasonably intuitive, easy to use, and providing players with explicit feedback. It is also visually appealing and can be customised to fit the game's aesthetic. Designers need to ensure a clear visual language is in place when a switch is active, as it can be ambiguous—both states must be clearly identified.

COLOUR THEORY AND CONTRAST

Colour and contrast are essential elements in UX and UI design. With a robust and strategic palette, designers can create visually appealing and effective interfaces that draw players' attention to crucial areas of the game.

The Basics

Humans learn colour naturally and inherently as they discover the world. Its intrinsic value and psychology are passively bestowed through our cultures, the natural world, and biology. The basic wheel consists of three primary colours (red, yellow, and blue), three secondary colours (created when primary colours are mixed: green, orange, and purple), and six tertiary colours (made from primary and secondary colours, such as blue-green or red-violet).

Colour theory studies colour interactions and how they can be used. It involves understanding their properties, such as hue, saturation, temperature, and brightness, and how they can be combined. A solid understanding of colour theory is essential for designers in any creative field, allowing them to establish visual appeal, convey meaning, be culturally appropriate, and evoke emotions.

Colour Terminology

RGB is a colour model that combines different intensities of red, green, and blue light to create various colours used in digital and electronic devices. Each colour is represented by a combination of red, green, and blue values ranging from 0 to 255. For example, white (whole light) is described as (255, 255, 255), and black (absence of light) is defined as (0, 0, 0).

Hue refers to the purest and most basic form of a colour. The attribute enables us to distinguish it as red, blue, green, yellow, or any other colour on the visible spectrum.

Saturation refers to the intensity of a colour. A highly saturated colour is pure and vivid. A desaturated colour adds more grey or white, making it less intense.

Value (lightness) refers to the quantity of light seen in colour. Higher numbers produce brighter colours, while lower values produce darker ones.

Shade refers to a hue that has been darkened by adding black to it.

Tint refers to a colour that has been lightened by adding white.

Tone refers to the addition of black and white (grey).

A **hex code** is a six-digit code that represents a specific colour. It's used in digital design to ensure consistency across different platforms and devices. Each digit in the hex code represents a different colour channel.

Temperature refers to a colour's perceived warmth or coolness and can create specific moods. Warm colours like red, orange, and yellow are associated with heat and evoke excitement and energy. In contrast, cool colours like blue, green, and purple are associated with calmness and relaxation.

Colour Schemes and Combinations

A **complementary** colour scheme involves using two colours opposite each other on the colour wheel. This creates a high contrast, attention-drawing, and visually pleasing effect. Designers can use this scheme to highlight essential elements to make them stand out.

A **monochromatic** colour scheme uses different shades, tints, and tones of the same colour. It makes a cohesive and harmonious look and can reduce visual clutter.

An **analog (or analogous)** colour scheme selects only one dominant hue and complements it with other hues adjacent to it on the colour wheel. Analogous colour schemes can help create low-contrast, calm, or subdued artwork that can help reduce eye strain and fatigue.

A **split complementary** colour scheme uses a base colour and two colours adjacent to its complement. The scheme provides diverse colour options while maintaining a balance of warm and cool colours.

A **triad** colour scheme uses three evenly spaced colours on the colour wheel.

Colour Psychology

There is more to choosing colours for the UI than just picking what you like. Colours have different meanings. Some people don't even physically see colour the same way. Various countries and cultures give colours different emotional and psychological meanings. There is nothing I can't abide more than single-minded thinking when someone categorically states that *this* colour means *this*. Saying *"Red means bad"* is reductive.

Colour psychology studies how colours can impact human behaviour, emotions, and feelings. So when someone says, *"Red means bad,"* they are being biased. Yes, games use a lot of red to symbolise enemies, health, pain, and death, but it can equally be used for luck, love, and excitement. People don't avoid the red carpet. The point is to not be absolute in your thinking; otherwise, you can fall into the trap of monotony. Furthermore, colour won't save bad UX or confusing interactions.

What is more constructive is to define a colour swatch language. Brand your colours. Select words based on usage and association (practical or emotional), and then use them regularly throughout the game. For example, if the game needs an "alert" colour, we want a consistent, vibrant colour that players will immediately react to when they see it. In RPGs (pole-playing games), loot is often colour-coded to denote value and scarcity. We don't say *yellow* loot (yellow or orange are frequently used for the rarest items); we say, wait for it, *legendary.*

Here are some commonly associated psychological meanings behind colours:

- **Red:** passion, love, excitement, danger, energy, vitality, luck, happiness
- **Orange:** energy, enthusiasm, warmth, creativity, youth, warmth
- **Yellow:** joy, hope, optimism, expensive, construction
- **Green:** nature, growth, harmony, wealth
- **Blue:** calm, trust, security, intelligence
- **Purple:** royalty, luxury, creativity, spirituality
- **Black:** sophistication, elegance, power, mourning
- **White:** purity, innocence, peace, minimalism, simplicity

The different meanings behind colours can help designers create unique designs. However, their meanings are not definitive either. There are several games where the entire UI is red. Sure, some commonly recognised standards exist, but we can often redefine them in a game. What is important is being consistent with the language. We all perceive colour differently; our perception and cultural biases change how we view and understand colour psychologically (or philosophically)—equally, some people physically see them differently.

Colour Vision Deficiency

Colour vision deficiency (CVD) or colour blindness is a condition where individuals cannot distinguish specific colours. It affects roughly one in twelve men and one in two hundred women. Worldwide, it is estimated that there are about 300 million individuals with colour blindness[1]. It's primarily genetic and inherited, though it can also result from diseases such as diabetes. It can also be a symptom of ageing, drugs, and medications. There are different types of colour blindness, and most colour-blind people cannot fully see red, green, or blue light. In sporadic cases, some people cannot see any colour.

Protanopia makes distinguishing between red and green hard, while deuteranopes struggle with greens and reds, and tritanopes have difficulty perceiving blue. Monochromacy, also known as achromatopsia, is a rare genetic condition in which individuals cannot see any colours, and the world appears in shades of grey due to the absence or malfunction of cones in the retina needed for colour vision.

This is important to know because it means that the colours you select don't mean anything by themselves. It would be best if you had solutions that allow players to complete the functions of the game without the need for colour, either by augmenting them, supporting them with other stimuli, or avoiding the need for them altogether. *Making something just go red is not a good UX solution!*

One of the most common solutions is providing different colour palettes for each condition. Players can switch palettes to differentiate game elements such as player names, reticles, enemy markers, and anything else that provides information during gameplay. Some games also allow players to adjust specific colours by using a colour wheel or colour picker for each element, which is one of the best solutions you can do.

What you want to avoid is full-screen filters. These filters will make a blanket change to the entire frame, which then tweaks *all* the colours in the frame. It's like putting on sunglasses that change the world's colours, and now everything you know looks strange, and equally, the various elements that use colour for gameplay information are still hard to see. If the source colours aren't well selected, adding an overlay furthers the confusion. The problem with this approach is that it attempts to *fix* CVD instead of designing a solution that makes it irrelevant.

Colour Mistakes and Best Practises

- Stop using or trying to implement colour-blind filters. Seriously.
- Never rely on colour alone.
- Textures on UI can make a colour feel different than intended.
- Make sure the contrast with text is high enough to be readable.
- Monochromatic UI can work if done correctly.
- Your colour choice can influence how people play.

- If you ever meet someone whose go-to solution is *"just make it go red,"* immediately take three deep breaths and ask them, *"What if you can't see red?"* Study their response. You will learn a lot about this person.
- Don't add colour if it's going to confuse interactions.
- Don't use too many colours. Too many can quickly make your design look unintentionally chaotic, cluttered, and unprofessional. As a rule of thumb, limit your colour palette to two to four colours. Tints, tones, and shades can create variations and harmony.
- Ignoring colour theory.
- CVD, colour blindness, low vision, and dyslexia must be considered from the outset.
- Not considering the context of where your colour will be used.

Contrast

Contrast is balance and the difference between elements. Humans are naturally drawn to differences, so utilising this contrast can help create hierarchy and enhance visual appeal. The primary action on the interface should have the most contrast. Therefore, designers must use contrast strategically and thoughtfully to achieve the best results. For example, using a dark background with light text creates a high contrast, making the text stand out and easy to read. Similarly, using a large bold font for a headline and a smaller font for body text creates contrast in size, defining which is more important in the relationship.

Various elements can create contrast. **Colour** can create emphasis, highlight important information, and make the design visually appealing. Designers can exploit dark and light colours, different intensities, diverse hues, and different temperatures. The difference in **size** between different elements can create a hierarchy and make the design more dynamic. The difference in **shape** can create emphasis and add interest. The difference in **texture** between elements is compelling in conveying a mood or emotion. Varying the horizontal, vertical, diagonal, and radial **positions** of elements between elements can help differentiate them from each other and make a visually exciting layout.

Interfaces require the proper contrast for usability and engagement, but overusing it creates clutter and confusion. The Web Content Accessibility Guidelines (WCAG) have many recommendations for contrast in digital documents and devices[2]. In addition, you can use colour contrast checks online to test your chosen colours[3].

TYPOGRAPHY

Typography is the voice of your interface and your game—besides the main characters growling at each other. It's the technique of arranging type to make written language legible, readable, and appealing while conveying tone and brand identity. It involves selecting appropriate typefaces and utilising the different fonts within. Once selected, designers can manipulate font sizes, weights, and orientations to convey information and enhance the visual appeal.

What Is a Typeface?

A typeface is a set of design features for letters and other characters, such as the presence or absence of a serif, the letters' weight, spacing, and the height difference between upper- and lowercase letters. Typefaces are categorised based on their style. For denser text, opting for a serif or a sans-serif font that can handle the heavy lifting is better.

Serif typefaces have a slight projection finishing off a stroke of a letter—twiddly bits. These typefaces and fonts evoke a classic, refined, and sophisticated feel.

Sans serif typefaces (sans as in the French for *without*) don't have serifs. It often appears more informal and relaxed.

Decorative typefaces are more fun and eye-catching than others, but they may not be well-suited for body text, where they become challenging to read. They can be great for headers, but choose wisely, as they often don't provide great language support and can make an interface look low-quality or gimmicky.

Script typefaces resemble cursive handwriting. Like decorative fonts, they can be tricky to read at smaller sizes and generally don't offer great language support. However, they can be an excellent choice to convey a sense of personalised, handcrafted branding. It's best to reserve them for your logo or headers.

Fonts and Formatting

A font is the variation in weight and size of a typeface. So, if the typeface is *Calibri*, the different weights, bold, italic, and condensed are fonts.

Tracking

Tracking is adjusting the space between characters in a block of text. Designers use tracking to modify the overall spacing uniformly, affecting the text's density and readability. Adjusting this to certain extremes can affect the tone of words.

Kerning

Kerning refers to the amount of space between individual characters. By adjusting the kerning, we can fix any issues with specific fonts. However, be careful; you can adjust too much and make things look wonky.

Leading

Leading (also known as line spacing) is the adjustment of the distance between two or more adjacent lines of type. Increasing this value can help space out larger blocks of text so they can appear more readable.

Cap-Height

Cap-height refers to the distance between the baseline and the top of the capital letters. A taller cap-height can make the text appear more prominent and easier to read, while a shorter cap-height can make the text appear more compact and condensed.

X-Height

X-height refers to the distance between the baseline and the top of the lower-case letters, excluding the ascenders and descenders. A font's x-height is the vertical distance from its baseline to the top of the lowercase letters x, v, w, and z. Rounded letters such as d, p, r, and e extend just above the x-height line and below the baseline. The x-height is crucial when selecting a typeface, as a higher x-height can make the text appear more open and accessible to read, while a lower x-height can make the text appear more condensed and compact.

Uppercase

THIS IS UPPER CASE. It can appear quite "shouty" when not used appropriately. It can work well for headers and elements that need to be, well ... shouty, for example, if the player is running low on health or needs to reload. It can become challenging to read if used for large bodies of text.

Lowercase

It can be used stylistically or can look like an error.

Title Case

The first letter of every major word is capitalised, For example, Hello World.

Sentence Case

Sentence case is where the first letter of the first word in a sentence is capitalised, along with any proper nouns or other words that would usually be capitalised. Sentence case is commonly used when writing for books, articles, and large bodies of UI text.

Selecting UI Fonts

Selecting the right fonts is critical.

When making your choices, you will need to decide three things:

1. What will be your main text (body) font?
2. What font will you use for headings?
3. Do you need a special font for accents, decoration, style, captions, quotations, specific accessibility needs, and callouts?

These are a few extra tips to keep in mind.

- Ensure your header and body text fonts look right together if they are from different typefaces.
- Don't use too many fonts.
- Most fonts require licenses to be used commercially. Some are free but may still need permission and credit.
  - Always keep a record of the fonts you are using and where you got them from.
  - A license does not necessarily transfer from one project to the next.
- Ensure your fonts are thematically in keeping with your project. Stylish fonts can be a fun addition and make your headers stand out. However, ensure your body font is your "workhorse," meaning it is clear and can do a lot of heavy lifting.
- Never, on any account, use a font that is the basis of a Wordmark Logo (a text-based logo where the name of the company or brand

uses a unique font). Just because you can download the Disney font doesn't mean you can use it.

- Define a font usage guide. A balance of set sizes and weight usage can help keep your design clean and reduce cognitive load.
- Depending on the font, text below 18 pt can become highly unreadable.
- Different font weights help create contrast and hierarchy. Use a couple of different weights, and try to vary between two to three weights. So use regular and semi-bold instead of regular and medium.

Internationalisation

Localising for other languages means that your font must also support all the various characters (glyphs) each language may need. If your chosen font cannot do this (and most don't), you will need to either use a Unicode font, edit the existing font, or have the technology to switch to one that does.

Here are a few tips to assist localisation teams when developing UI that houses long strings:

- Provide maximum character limits for fixed-size text fields.
- Add notes with strings that add context to help localisation teams create more accurate translations.
- Allow for a 40% character buffer in your layouts for localisation, as translations vary in length.
- String concatenation is a handy feature to implement when variables dynamically change in a text field, but the results can sometimes not translate meaningfully. For example, when translated, [Legendary] [Sword] may end up reading strangely in other languages.
- If it doesn't exist, request a debug tool to preview languages for easy testing.

ICONOGRAPHY

Iconography uses symbols, glyphs, or icons to represent functions or actions. These icons are often used in place of text or to support it. Icons offer **clarity** by providing a clear and concise representation of various functions or actions, making it easier for users to understand and navigate the interface. Additionally, icons contribute to **efficiency** as they can save space and reduce clutter by replacing lengthy text descriptions with a single visual element. Moreover, icons have a **universal appeal** as they can be easily recognised and understood by users from different cultures and languages, making them a valuable tool for creating interfaces accessible to a global audience.

Icons can pose challenges due to potential ambiguity, cultural offence, or lack of recognition. Designers must diligently select universally understood and consistent icons throughout the interface to avoid misinterpretation. Some icons are unique to the brand or even the game's mechanics, and it's perfectly fine to introduce new symbology as long as they are thoroughly introduced and supported with heuristic descriptions.

How to Design 'Good' Icons

- Icons need to work in multiple sizes. If you make everything massive and detailed, you can be disappointed when scaling them down. Sometimes, the engine can handle the scaling, but often, it's more efficient to make a smaller version with optimised detail.
- The icon's stroke width or fill amount should match the typography when possible.
- Use pixel grids and guides to ensure it's pixel-perfect to avoid "half pixels."
- Reduce your iconography to its simplest form. The more complex or noisy it is, the longer it takes to comprehend.
- Research familiar tropes and representations. A mechanical gear icon is widely used for Options menus. You can change things, but if it makes it complicated to understand, is it worth it?
- Test your icons with people without context and ask them, "What does this mean?" If they can answer correctly, you have a robust and influential icon.

LAYOUT

It can be a struggle to get everything to fit and read well in a composition. However, you can do a few things to help the layout and information flow.

Alignment

Whether a simple wireframe or a fully finalised project, ensuring clean and effective alignment is crucial in achieving a harmonious balance of aesthetics and functionality, even if the style is purposefully punk and chaotic. Alignment is the process of positioning and arranging elements in relation to one another. Proper alignment establishes a hierarchy, with critical components in prominent positions, and ensures elements are easy to read, understand, and interact with. In addition to visual alignment, designers also need to consider functional alignment—the process of aligning elements with their purpose.

You want to constantly look for lines of continuation and ways to connect the dots for a precise reading path. In the West, we typically read left to right and top to bottom. This is not the case in all countries. Creating multiple layouts for various regions can be impractical, expensive, or artistically limiting. Typically, the game's target market dictates the design. Use the tools in your software packages to ensure clean and consistent alignment. Even if it's a rough mockup, five minutes of shuffling elements into place can help improve the overall impression you want.

Rhythm and Variety

Rhythm and variety play a significant role in how engaging content is. The more appealing the layout, the more likely players will spend time exploring it. **Rhythm** involves the repetition of design elements such as shapes, colours, and textures to create a pleasing visual pattern, making the UI feel cohesive and unified. On the other hand, **variety** introduces different design elements to add *islands of detail* and prevents the UI from feeling too predictable or dull.

When working with long text segments, it's good to break them up or complement them with images, videos, quotes, and bullet points. This quickly changes the rhythm and provides little breaks when reading. When used effectively, players will appreciate an aesthetically pleasing and functional design that uses rhythm and variety, but too much can make a design look disjointed and inconsistent.

Lines of Force

These invisible lines guide the player's eye along visual pathways to help dictate the reading path and develop a sense of movement and flow. They provide vital focal points and hierarchy, directing users to important information or actions. Usually, the lines start from your screen's topmost navigation point and then offset vertically with each new information block. Sometimes, these lines can be diagonal. Imagine drawing lines through your layouts and noting what connections you make. Try to picture how the player's eye will follow these lines and ask yourself, "Are you leading them down the right path, and are they hitting the right points?"

Anchoring

Anchoring refers to fixing certain elements in a specific location on the screen via the centre or corners of a widget. The layout will inform you of the appropriate anchoring of your components. This technique ensures that when elements move or change, either due to text changes, screen adjustments, or animations, they adhere to the layout and all the vital work we have done with readability, flow, and hierarchy. For example, anchoring a widget to the bottom right of the HUD (like a mini-map) means that if the screen size changes vertically or horizontally, the element will remain in that corner.

Most game engines have systems to define where the anchor is—either one of the nine points of the screen or a custom axis. Anchors can also take up all four corners of the screen or spread vertically or horizontally from top to bottom. There is a lot of creative flexibility in how you anchor. It's essential to ensure that you anchor from the primary parent downwards and consider how the anchoring will vary based on the type of screen. Through testing, observing how things move when the content inside expands and retracts or the viewport changes.

Padding

Padding is the space between UI elements or between the contents of an element's border. It can be measured vertically and horizontally. Always use more padding than you need. It will help make your presentation look more luxurious and maintain it when things with variable heights and widths change the layout.

ANIMATION

Motion can enhance aesthetics and UX. Animation can convey feedback with more adjacency, contrast, and tone, allowing elements to grab attention. It can be as simple as a subtle pulse on a notification, massive sweeping transitions, or bouncy buttons. Some ambient motion can bring a static screen to life, and a little spinning icon can help reassure players that the game hasn't crashed.

Spending a little time learning how to animate, even to a basic level, for simple micro-interactions and transitions will benefit the effectiveness of your designs.

Realtime vs Non-real-time Interactions

The *state* of something is fundamentally static, while the *act* is temporal and based on motion. A UI element can be in the state of being animated or in the act of being animated. The timing of an interaction can be categorised as either real-time or non-real-time. Real-time interactions involve direct player engagement, while non-real-time interactions occur after a player's action and are transitional in nature. If a player freely scrolls through text, the movement would be in real time, allowing for immediate manipulation. In contrast, pressing a button triggers a premade animation that changes to another state.

Working with Animation

Animations are created by manipulating an object's properties and values over time or looping them indefinitely. Using particular techniques and principles, the animator adds tone, style, and a brand signature.

The principles are a hierarchical rule set, a collection of styles, philosophies and ideas that define the manipulations, and techniques that specify how the animations look and make us feel. Properties are the specific object parameters that are being manipulated. These include (and are not limited to) position, opacity, scale, rotation, anchor point, colour, stroke width, and shape. Values are the actual numeric property.

Understanding how players perceive motion is essential. When setting up an animation, you need to understand and clearly define its purpose. What information is this motion helping to convey? It's not just about adding *pizzazz*; it has more practical implications. There is an expectation of how an object behaves and what is expected. It adds value to the underlying usability, accessibility, and experience by creating continuity, narrative, and relationships that form between objects when they animate together, creating hierarchical connections that help players understand and make decisions.

Easing

This motion reinforces 'naturalism' and creates a sense of consistent continuity. Object behaviours mimic how players expect real-world objects to accelerate and decelerate over time.

Offset and Delay

Designers can use offset and delay to define elements' roles and importance, subconsciously suggesting these objects have a story to tell. For example, your main header slides in and is sequentially followed by the subheader, which infers their hierarchy. As elements animate with an offset, it directs us to read the last line, often a button or action.

Parenting

Parenting creates object relationships and hierarchies that link the properties of one element to the properties of others (the child). When an objective moves, it may be set up in a way that also triggers motion or a change in another object.

Transformation

An object turns into another, like a circle morphing into a square. Transformation is the most discernible because our brains notice it.

Value Change

A value change communicates the dynamic nature of data and informs players that the data is interactive. If these values were purely static, not only would this relationship get lost, but we would lose the opportunity to make players feel something. Think about the joy that comes from watching your combo metre go up with each consecutive punch.

Masking

Masking something is well-established in graphic design circles, but this is static. When in motion, the relationship between the shape and the object creates continuity by what is revealed or concealed. Clicking on a thumbnail image or video may expand to reveal it was just a mask of a more extensive background, continuing that connection.

Overlay

Overlays allow designers to place one layer over another, changing the value of both. They allow hiding or revealing information based on player needs or actions.

Cloning

Cloning is about creating continuity, relationship, and narrative when new objects originate and depart in motion. New objects are made from an existing one to drive user attention and focus.

Obscuration

Try to think of obscuration as the *act* of being obscured and not the *state* of being obscured. This can be as simple as blurring the background as you transition between screens or displaying a modal to clarify what is now in focus.

Parallax

When two or more elements move simultaneously but at different speeds, the most critical interactive elements are the fastest.

Dimensionality

Manipulating two-dimensional elements and spatial changes can imply that elements have different sides, some in three dimensions, which can suggest a link. Take a UI card that you can flip around or slide out of view. The usability links to real-world affordances people are familiar with and expect.

Dolly and Zoom

Dolly and Zoom are film industry-related concepts that refer to moving objects relevant to the camera. The principle refers to the player feeling like they are travelling through elements spatially, though it's a manipulation of uniform scale, revealing greater options or details.

AUDIO

We often consider visual elements the only means of providing information, but sound is just as important. It enhances immersion, provides feedback, and contributes to the overall mood. Different notes, chords, tempos, rhythms, accents, and cadences can change how someone feels and provide valuable feedback. Does it sound negative or positive? Does it rise in pitch and tempo to imply concluding? Do we need to honk the horn when a player does something wrong or ignite a whole orchestra when they achieve something great?

Designing distinct and recognisable sounds for different actions or events can help users understand the interface more intuitively. Ambient sounds, background music, and spatial audio can create an engaging and immersive player experience that contributes to the overall atmosphere and immersion in the game.

Consideration should be given to making the audio elements accessible to all players. This includes providing visual cues or alternatives for important audio information, especially for players with hearing impairments. Allowing players to adjust the volume levels, turn specific audio elements on/off, or customise audio settings according to their preferences can enhance their overall experience.

WORKFLOW

Every studio has a different workflow, and access to technology will vary. You must understand how a place operates, convert yourself into it, and hopefully improve it if necessary. You can bring several practices from job to job to help maintain good workflows and organisation, at least for yourself.

Organisation

Naming Conventions

A naming convention is a set of rules for choosing consistent and readable names for variables, functions, files, and other system entities. It helps developers understand and work with file storage and structure. Many developers have different takes on this, so it's essential to be flexible and follow the conventions the studio has in place.

General rules for naming conventions:

1. Only use Latin characters and numbers (avoid special characters).
2. Have a consistent case. Be it Lowercase, Camel, Snake, or Honeybadger.
3. No spaces. You can use _, but some code bases don't like it.
4. All numbers should start with a zero (e.g. 01, 02, 03). There is no point in adding additional zeros in front of an element unless you go to that digit count. It just adds unnecessary complexity, for example: 001, 002, 003, but you only have eight items.

Recommended Example

"Event_EventSpecific_Element_Type_Variation.extension"

- *Event* is a two- or three-character identifier for what this element is used for. For example, FE stands for front-end.
- *Event specific* is an additional identifier related to the previous. For example, FE_Settings_
- *Element* is a short identifier for the type of component it is; say, it's a background image, we call it BG or, if it's a texture, just T.
- *Type* helps identify specifically what type of element it is.
- *Variation* is the number identifier for a group of items, for example, 01, 02, 03.
- *Extension* is the computer file type, which you can choose but not in terms of formatting and text.

Folder Structure

Suitable folder structures are essential for organising and managing files efficiently.

- Plan and organise folders based on the type of content and its intended use
- Use clear and descriptive folder names to make it easy to locate specific files
- Establish a logical hierarchy to categorise files and subfolders, making navigation intuitive
- Avoid creating too many levels of nesting to prevent excessive complexity
- Consistently apply the folder structure across projects or departments to maintain uniformity
- Regularly review and update the folder structure to accommodate changes in file organisation needs
- Consider including a readme file or documentation explaining the folder structure for new users or team members

Performance

If you work closely with the engine and do not simply deliver assets or mockups for someone else to implement, you may be required to help improve performance. You can't just make an incredibly high-resolution flip book animated texture and expect it to perform well at runtime. System and graphic memory have limits, so we have a budget for textures used and computations made. It's vital to utilise the correct texture resolutions and space-saving techniques such as channel packing, materials, signed distance fields, and nine-slicing to break down textures to get more out of less. The "Power of Two" rule is essential for game development because game engines process data in limited chunks for efficiency. Adhering to this rule ensures that images are as efficient as possible while providing an excellent visual experience.

Game Engines and Software

If you only work in graphic design and static art, I implore you to learn the fundamentals of bringing your artwork into the game engine. It will enhance your skills and give you more control over how things look in the final product.

Most companies will grant you access to the latest software licenses, or you can request them. If you are working freelance, indie, or on a budget, there are free versions of most photo manipulation, illustration, wireframe, organisation, and prototyping software.

Games companies will use a third-party engine like Unreal Engine or Unity or have a proprietary engine. Both have their unique advantages and disadvantages. With third-party engines, you will find a plethora of information from the developer and online resources from other users to help you in using it. In-house software won't have this luxury—however, the people who made it will be in the building and usually have internal documentation. Also, if you require a feature that isn't currently part of the in-house engine and there is a project justification for its need, it may be straightforward for them to add it in a way that works best for your workflow.

NOTES

1 colourblindawareness.org/colour-blindness
2 w3.org/TR/WCAG21
3 webaim.org/resources/contrastchecker

Presentation Matters

8

HARD TRUTHS

Like it or not, you are a brand. We dress a certain way, feel strongly about specific issues, and, as much as we say we don't care, we want to be seen in a particular light. We don't all go out of our way to sell ourselves as a "brand" in our personal lives, but standing out when applying for a role (especially at the start) requires us to appear as a viable candidate. How you appear on paper and your actions make a difference in how you are perceived. This is the same on the other side of the table. The studios care about how their brand looks as an employer and will throw all sorts of perks and "culture" at candidates to attract the best ones.

How you present yourself does matter. Your personality, values, work, experiences, and even the questions and answers in an interview all amalgamate into your 'brand.' I've interviewed many UI/UX candidates (people who specialise in information presentation); if you can't present yourself well, how will you do it well for the game?

If you are finding your first job or applying for a new one, we must acknowledge a few things first. The following is not intended to discourage you. Managing your expectations and being honest with yourself through this process are crucial. Keep a level head, and be all you can be.

Not every role matches what you know you can do or expect. Every studio and individual has a different perception of 'talent' and "good." You believe you are perfect for a role, but you may still get rejected, and that's okay (we'll talk about dealing with rejection later).

After you apply, many factors are at play. Numerous people will review it, and not everyone shares the same opinions and perspectives. They're human, too, and subject to the same life and professional pressures we all

DOI: 10.1201/9781003367116-8

experience. They may have a stack of candidates to review and very little time, so we've got to grab their attention. You will compete not only with the other candidates but with factors entirely out of your control, such as internal politics, nepotism, chaos theory, and unforeseeable events of 'Force Majeure.' Don't waste energy over things outside your control that you can only speculate about.

We all want to work at our dream studio and game. But remember to be humble and realistic. You may have to get what you can if it's your first job. If you don't have much experience, getting some "skin in the game" will be more beneficial than waiting for that one dream to happen. Make *this* moment now your dream. There is nothing wrong with where you start because we all start somewhere.

CVS AND RÉSUMÉS

A curriculum vitae (CV) translates from Latin as 'the course of (one's) life' and acts as a 'Wikipedia' list of all your achievements. The term résumé (resume or resumé), is predominantly used in the USA. Regardless, it doesn't matter what the thing you send is called, but that the thing you send—*your first impression*—doesn't suck.

People skim-read and don't have the time to read multiple pages about everything you've ever done. It's not because they're rude or uninterested; it's just their time to review candidates is finite, and the number of candidates is often expansive. I'm not knocking your accomplishments, but ask yourself what is relevant here and which will help secure you an interview. It's not just about what you did, but how. What was the result, and what did you learn? The information you hand over needs to be relevant to the interaction.

One of the hardest things about preparing a CV is cutting the bullshit. It's essential to focus on substance, not length. A straightforward one- or two-pager is best. Avoid a repetitive document filled with filler and fluff. Strike a balance between crucial and concise. Each piece of information should add value, and it's essential not to skimp on critical projects or achievements. Use keywords and language strategically that reflects the needs of the job specification. Display your personality by sharing side projects and hobbies relevant to your profession. Highlight your continued learning. Quantify achievements with tangible data. Be specific about your involvement in projects. It's the difference between saying you *have* a skill and *showing* it.

Writing Tips

Studios create job applications not because they want to fill a seat or hire someone for the hell of it. They have a specific production need and cannot solve it with their current workforce or resources. Constructing a CV is the ultimate information architecture project—if a UI or UX designer can't make an aesthetically pleasing and effective CV, it can raise concerns. The following tips have been provided to help you do just that.

1. We're not writing a novel, so don't bloat your content with jargon or complex descriptions. Keep it brief and to the point. Keep your CV to one or two pages.
2. Curate your content to suit the organisation and the job you are applying for—every time.
3. Be honest and explicit in your goals and requirements.
4. Be clear about your values and experiences.
5. Validate your skills rather than announce them. Show what you learnt.
6. Don't be afraid to show your personality. It will help make your CV more engaging and memorable. It's what makes you, *you*. Keep it professional, of course.
7. Never score your abilities with progress bars, star ratings, or anything that 'gamifies' your skills. So, tell me, where did you get that *nine out of ten* in Photoshop? Does that mean when you hit ten, you have completed it? If you did a course in an application and got a qualification, excellent, say that. You can list something as a skill and say you are *experienced with* or have *some knowledge* of an area. It will show you as modest and eager to learn more.
8. Don't stress about writing in either the third or first person; worry about the clarity of the content.
9. You don't need to include a photo. It takes up space you could be using for something else.
10. Check your spelling and grammar. It might sound petty, and people can forgive the odd mistake. However, most software has checks for this. If you have challenges with writing or writing in another language, there is software that can help, and you can always ask a friend or mentor to proofread.
11. Seriously, never use an icon of a *human brain* and say it's one of your skills. I've experienced this with someone I interviewed. It was situated along with all the other skills icons like Adobe software, Figma, and even a pencil. It just screamed arrogance, an impression

you don't want your CV to give off. *"You have a brain!? Amazing! We've been looking for someone with one of those!"*

12. It's okay to include hobbies as little icebreakers, but something you include briefly in a personal statement.

13. Export your CV as a PDF unless your submission is via form or hosted on a personal website. Computers and phones handle them much better than anything else, and most PDF readers come with various features that make reviewing more accessible. You can't guarantee how the other formats will display the CV, and they may not have that specific software.

14. Ensure any links in your CV *work*, especially your **highly visible** portfolio link. If it's password-protected, embed it in the link. Reviewers often look at that first, so make it easy for them.

15. Your secondary school exam results are not relevant to include unless requested. Higher education and any professional certification are enough.

16. Don't use unsolicited references (people you haven't asked to give a reference).

17. It might sound prehistoric, but ensure your documents can be printed easily. It still happens, so a solid black background might not be practical.

18. Name your documents professionally. Include your full name, the document type (CV), and the job role being applied for. This will help with your professional presentation and organisation on their end.

PORTFOLIOS

A portfolio showcases a person's skills, experience, and accomplishments.

When applying for a UX job, you must demonstrate skills such as researching, user flows, wireframing, persona development, interaction design, and information architecture. For art and design jobs, much of the above is worth showing if you have it, in addition to interfaces, iconography, typography, motion graphics, and implementation examples.

I need to make this abundantly clear—to have the best chance of getting hired, the work in your portfolio needs to match or surpass the quality the game studio already produces. Be honest with yourself; if it's not yet there, you must keep working until it is. Re-focus the energy you would have spent on your CV and portfolio to create stronger portfolio assets.

Portfolio Rules

Having a great portfolio isn't just about having fantastic work, but also about how you show it. As you gain experience and grow your skills, so does the quality of the portfolio content. In either case, we must consider how we curate our content. Deciding which order to display pieces or which past work to exclude may challenge your biases and nostalgia. It's not easy, but remember, as much as the portfolio is about you, *it's not for you.*

With every new piece of work I add to my portfolio, I am still refining these **golden rules**.

#1 Only Show Your Best Work

For each piece, consider what skills it establishes and how well it demonstrates them. You will have to make some tough decisions. It's like picking which of your children is your favourite or breaking a hoarding habit; you must learn to let go. It's best to exclude certain items to make a positive impression. Anything you include in your portfolio can be asked about in an interview. You may stumble when questioned about something you made decades ago. Leave out projects that ended poorly or work you didn't enjoy (and it shows), as these can shape perceptions and lead to complex questions.

Remember, a portfolio is a tool for acquiring work, so if a piece of historical work isn't helping anymore, it must be *'put out to pasture.'* You can cherish the memories elsewhere. If you don't have much to show, it can be challenging to be selective and objective. If you don't have the pieces yet, you must keep working and making some.

#2 Curate the Experience

We want the reviewer (your audience) to travel through a curated experience where each element on display establishes a specific goal. Showcasing your *Satan Death Slayer 3* shooter icons before your cute and vibrant mobile game icons would indeed illustrate your range. However, it may not be the best element to start with when applying to a studio that only makes the latter game. With a bespoke approach, you generate a strategic path for your audience to follow.

#3 Presentation Matters

It raises concerns when an applicant focused on a UX or UI role cannot effectively present their work. Not only does your work need to look good, but how you present it should look good, too. Equally, the skill you demonstrate with each piece must be clearly illustrated. Employers will look at hundreds of portfolios, so you want to stand out for the right reasons. If challenges hinder your presentation, consider a prefabricated portfolio website.

#4 Consistency Is King

Ensure a familiar and consistent layout for each piece. It needs to look like the same person put it together. The reviewer shouldn't have to re-learn how to read your work. It looks more professional and establishes *your brand.*

#5 Show the Car First, Then "Under the Hood"

Always start with the money shot and then show your process. The journey can be very revealing. However, a reviewer will be less enthusiastic after reviewing all your decisions and assumptions to find the final product mediocre. Include wireframes, diagrams, pre-vis, and prototypes. Don't show photos of your sketchbooks and *"Pepe Silvia"* sticky note-encrusted walls. Ensure everything is re-created digitally.

#6 Be Professional

You are not always presenting *your* work. It may be work owned by your current or previous employer. It would be best to credit them by including the studio and game logos and copyright 'blurb.' If it's studio policy, ensure you have the items reviewed and approved. They may have specific layout requirements you must comply with. If you collaborated with other people, credit them and explain the division in responsibilities. Treat personal work similarly. Add a watermark or at least your name or social page.

#7 Control the Narrative

It's beneficial to support your portfolio pieces with a description. You don't need to write a book, embellish, lie, or undersell yourself. They may ask about what you wrote in an interview. Make it clear what your contribution was and, most importantly, what you learnt. This way, your readers don't make incorrect assumptions as you have set the story.

#8 Don't Fear Multimedia

Motion design is a significant UI skill, so don't shy away from including videos and GIFS. They take more effort to capture but add an extra dimension to your presentation and a fantastic demonstration of your abilities.

#9 Be Prepared

If the interview is on-site, check beforehand if they can show the portfolio in the room. Regardless, bring a laptop or tablet, just in case. For web-based portfolios, have the files saved to an offline source or in PDF format on an external device.

#10 Express Yourself

Yes, you are applying for a UI/UX job, but that doesn't mean including some off-topic work is wrong. Why not showcase examples of your personal projects, street art, or life drawing at the end of your presentation? It shows more of your personality, passion, and other skills a studio might find desirable. Don't worry if you don't have any extra stuff, but if you do and it looks good, why not show it?

Portfolio platforms

You work on your portfolio forever, so updating and iterating can't be a chore. How and where you show your portfolio depends on your resources and practicality, so consider your skills and the effort and time you can allocate. There is no point investing in a solution that becomes impractical to maintain. Equally, you must consider the reviewer's access to the content and readability. You may have the most outstanding content, but a reviewer who becomes frustrated accessing it will move on quickly.

Published Digital Document

Creating a digital document will give you complete creative control and freedom with layout, style, and flow. But remember, you are showing off your work *and* portfolio presentation—a bad presentation won't do you any favours. Building this document can take time, so focus on your strengths. Find a style you like, gather assets, design a layout, and create time-saving templates for each new piece of work. A well-constructed and optimised PDF will work on most computers and browsers, fit on most USB drives, and can be emailed or uploaded instantly. You can add links to video files, contact info, and social media.

Prefabricated

Due to professional and personal commitments, we may only find time to gather and prepare portfolio content but no time to build custom websites and hand-crafted documents. Understandably, a prefabricated creative social media platform (like Artstation or Behance) or template website would be preferable. I recommend checking the *WE CAN FIX IT IN UI* website for recommendations.

You upload images and descriptions, and the site handles the rest. These sites' social media aspects can increase organic discovery and create networking, freelance, and recruitment opportunities. Some platforms minimise social media and networking features but excel in presentation features. Be aware that your work online can be prone to digital theft and can be used in *degenerative* AI training. Include copyright information and watermarks in your project assets. Use privacy settings to safeguard yourself from thieves.

Custom Website

Building a custom portfolio website from scratch is an impressive but significant undertaking. Every aspect of the presentation meets your requirements and quality standards. Better yet, you can customise the experience for each potential employer. You can drive the flow of the conversation and dictate what information they see. It's an advanced option, so you must have adequate time, skills, and drive to make one. It would help if you made it easy to update, too. Submitting a custom website that looks and performs worse than a prefabricated one will not reflect well on your application.

Nothing to Show

Landing a position with little or no examples of professional experience can be a struggle. It can feel like a 'Catch-22'—the age-old, *I need experience so I can get a job so I can get experience* paradox. There are things you can do to help improve your chances.

Coursework

Initially, it's okay if most of your content is from higher education or a course. What matters is the quality of what you are showing. What does it demonstrate? Does it help or hinder? You need to carefully vet your content so it demonstrates the skills the employer seeks and doesn't detract. Editing this content can be demanding as you have an emotional attachment, but remember, the employer doesn't.

Even candidates with professional content would benefit from practising this. Does that older content now hinder the new stuff? You might appreciate the visible advancement in your skills over time, but the employer may make the distinction and judge it all as your current ability.

Highlight Your Transferable Skills

Some game job listings state they require "x years of experience." You can compensate for the lack of years with volunteer work, internships, and relevant work experience in a similar field. You could demonstrate how your education experience is transferable to the working world.

Ask for a Recommendation

Find a sponsor who knows you can do the job. Employee referrals can help a lot, and studios often have an automatic interview process for recommendations because they're trusted. Learning to network is essential, and this isn't an invitation to pester random game developers online. A sponsor will only make a recommendation if they feel confident in the skills and professionalism of the candidate.

Enthusiasm

You can't teach enthusiasm and passion. Show that you are excited and ready to learn and work. Get this positive energy across in your correspondence. Have an attitude that implies, "I don't know now, but I will soon," as opposed to, "I don't know how to do that."

Match the Culture

Show that you already embrace the company's values. This can be interpreted as sharing a positive attitude, expressing similar interests, or demonstrating teamwork values.

Accomplishments and Accolades

Where you have less experience, try showcasing worthwhile accomplishments and achievements you have been part of or have received.

Get Good at Software

You can make up for your professional experience with software. Train in emerging technology or desirable software that studios lack experienced developers proficient in. Become a technical expert in the studio's engine.

Personal Projects

Showing tutorials in a portfolio is okay, but it only illustrates that you can read and follow instructions, not problem-solving skills or creativity. Instead, use the tutorials to learn the basics, and then use those skills in personal projects. You want to focus on short, achievable, and creative assignments highlighting a specific ability. I stress the word *achievable*. Looking for a job and starting a career is stressful enough; shoving a mammoth project on top isn't going to help.

You can do 'case studies' of previous games. Analyse an existing title's experience design or art and how it could be improved. You could modernise the visual design of an older game or do an alternative take in a different genre. You could even make up your own game. Just be respectful of the game you are 'studying,' especially if it was made by the studio you are applying for. Equally, bonus points if you can tailor your custom artwork to be similar to the style and quality put out by that studio.

Studios look for 'published' work because it tells them you have experience with production processes and that they don't have to train as much. In short, it means less risk and reduced cost. However, any hiring manager or reviewer worth their title should be able to recognise raw skills, regardless of whether they're published or not. People have to start somewhere. If they were to look back on their career, someone must have had to take a risk on them at some point. You can train people in bureaucratic pipelines and production processes, but you can't teach passion, dedication, and a creative mind—only nurture them.

Game Jams

Relevant events can augment a lack of professional engagements. A 'Game Jam' is a short-term event (on location or online) where people worldwide gather in teams to create interactive experiences. It's an opportunity to develop and test your skills with like-minded developers. A successful project is magnificent to include as experience as it illustrates practical abilities, networking skills, and collaboration. There are free and paid events; you must factor in variable travel, food, and accommodation costs.

COVER LETTERS

Cover letters are considered a little "old hat," at least in the games industry. However, you can be asked to provide one for certain employers. This single-page document includes an introduction and a few paragraphs expressing your interest and requests that they consider your application. It is not a carbon copy 'add-on' you prefix all your applications with but a bespoke, personable, and carefully researched deceleration of intent.

Remember, you are delivering a sample of how *you* formally communicate—a professional indication of how you engage with an unfamiliar audience. More importantly, they gave you the tools to write this when posting the job advert. You have an example of how *they* speak. If you start writing in their voice, they will have a much easier time picturing you in the role at the studio.

Finally, please provide the correct links to your professional social media accounts. Prospective employers will likely check your social media, so ensuring your online presence reflects your professional brand is essential.

Cover Letter Template

Introduction Section

'Hello [Hiring Manager],'

Don't stress if you don't know their name; 'Hiring Manager' is acceptable. Many people may read it, skim it, or it goes through an automated process. Ensure you use preferred pronouns if they have published them; if not, use ungendered language. Also, using 'Dear' sounds old-fashioned, weird, and potentially offensive.

The introduction is crucial because we can't guarantee we will still have the reader's attention beyond the first paragraph. In this section, we will express our interest in the role, mention how we learnt about it, and briefly summarise our experience (let your CV do the rest).

'I would like to express my interest in the UI/UX something role at XYZ Studios.'

'I'm responding to the job post I saw on XYZ Studios' social media account.'

'I've been working in the industry for X years and at ZYX studios as a UI/UX something.'

Body

The 'Body' section is essential because it allows you to sell yourself and discuss your situation. Keep the language engaging and amusing if possible— divulge some exciting information about yourself, your interests, and your education. Remember to mirror the written language of the studio based on the job advert. Tell them what you have learnt and what you want to learn next. What impact might that bring to the role? Mention at least one specific thing that inspires you about the company or the games they make. Keep it genuine and concise; they can ask about it during the interview. We'll prove we are not a robot, discuss something we are proud of, and mention who referred us if they did.

> "I am a huge fan of how you approach character development in your games. When 'Character X' rescues 'Character Y' from the burning house, even though they are enemies, it moves me to my core."

Conclusion

Now, the easy part. Thank them for their time, and provide your contact details and professional social media links. Ensure your links work, and your social media profile name is appropriate. End with:

> 'All the best.'
> 'YOUR NAME'

Dig Deep

9

APPLYING FOR JOBS

Okay, you've got your degree and a certificate and are looking for your next gig. You've prepared your CV and portfolio. What is the best way to find jobs? It can be challenging even with the right skills and education; candidates must proceed through various interview stages, tests, and scrutiny. What's available out there depends on the economic climate and the industry's present state. It's not all fun and games.

Where to Start

I am not a professional recruiter. Shocking, I know. I can't secure you a job immediately after reading this book, nor give you the recipe for a 100% success rate with acquiring them. I can only prepare and guide you as best I can.

Before you start your search, consider what is important to you—your values. You must carefully weigh your survival needs, desires, and what you are willing to compromise on. It doesn't matter what stage you're at in your career; consider these points ahead of your search.

Ask yourself what matters most: rewards, culture, projects, autonomy, mentorship, or experience opportunities. You need a realistic idea of what you want and are willing to compromise. It's rare to find something 'perfect' that ticks off all the boxes. While you may not be able to have everything, being realistic about your job preferences can lead to a more satisfying situation.

- What kind of perks and compensation do I need?
- What are you willing to sacrifice?
- Can I relocate or only work remotely?
- What size studio? Do I want to work on AAA or indie games?

DOI: 10.1201/9781003367116-9

- Is there a specific technology you want to focus on? (e.g. mobile, consoles, or VR)
- Do you need any job right now because they are about to shut the lights off?

We all have different priorities and responsibilities. We might not have the luxury of being picky right now and only work at the flashy place with an imported Italian expresso machine and faux grass carpet (which is probably toxic anyway.) You may be in a dire position and simply want the most significant pay compensation you can get and job security. It might be the start of your career, and it's a *'take what you can get'* situation. At the very least, we want somewhere where they treat you like a human and provide space to learn and grow. We all deserve that much, at least.

Finding Jobs and How to Apply

Finding a job in the games industry is highly competitive and challenging, even with relevant qualifications and experience. A studio may only need one UX designer (if at all), so job availability is already limited, yet the competition for it is significant. More common jobs have more openings, but the candidate pool is still oversubscribed and competitive. It feels untenable sometimes.

Don't give up hope. It's essential to hustle and be proactive at this stage. Continue working on your portfolio whilst applying for jobs you find, even if you don't feel entirely qualified. If you wait until you think you're ready, you might miss your chance. However, be selective and apply for roles that genuinely interest you and align with your goals. Applying for every single job you see, regardless if it's right for you, can lead to unnecessary stress, rejection, and wasted time. We want to maintain a focus on what we want but are open to pathways we may not have considered depending on how we answered the earlier questions.

Some higher education courses can lead to your first gig, be it an internship or junior position. If that is not the case, an excellent place to begin is with a website like *gamedevmap.com*. These sites present a map displaying almost every known studio worldwide. Each map marker contains a link to a studio's website (which will include their open positions) and information on what type of developer they are. This could be your first roadblock. If you cannot relocate, and remote options are not available or possible, these studios in your area may be your only options for now. Remember, just because you have access to a vast database doesn't mean you should blanket apply to every studio on Earth. Finding a job may feel like a lottery sometimes, but how you apply to them shouldn't be treated like buying a stack of scratch cards, either.

Job Websites and Career Pages

A good starting point can be platforms like *LinkedIn*, *Glassdoor*, and other job boards. Most of these sites let you set up alerts based on your career interests. Use these sites to find out about jobs, but don't use the "easy apply" function; this automated function takes away your adjacency and control and often means your "application" is in some spam folder somewhere. Find the details and contacts you need, and apply under your terms. Discord communities like *UIPeeps.com* and WE CAN FIX IT IN UI frequently announce jobs, too.

Game studios have dedicated career pages on their official websites. These are (usually) up-to-date lists of all their open positions with direct ways to apply, either with an email address or form. Most studios allow for a speculative application if you don't see a listing for your desired role. This will enable you to apply, and the studio will keep your information on file if something comes up (as long as they are legally permitted) or create a role based on their need for your skills. It's not a guarantee, but with the right candidate, they may consider it.

Studios also announce jobs on social media. So, even if you *hate* social media, creating a professional account to follow studios and related accounts can be advantageous. Ensure you *read* their posting carefully, as applying may require a specific contact. Failure to follow the instructions may hurt your application, as you will be seen as not interpreting communications correctly, or the application system might discard it automatically.

Be cautious if approaching game developers directly on social media. The majority are not rude if they ignore you; some are sworn not to communicate with the public. Many will hopefully direct you to the correct contact or pass on your portfolio if it's good, but don't expect someone who has never worked with you to vouch for you. If direct communication is solicited, it can be an excellent opportunity for networking and mentoring. Be polite and respectful; developers are people, too, not to mention potential future colleagues.

Internships

As discussed in Chapter 3, internships can sometimes be arranged after higher education or applied for at particular studios. They present an excellent opportunity to build connections and gain experience, but remember, they are highly competitive.

Apprenticeships

It's challenging to work directly in a studio without any experience. Apprenticeships are a viable option to help build relative expertise if they are in similar fields like creative media, a web, or IT business. Higher education establishments can help you find something, or you can search online and on local government sites that help with employment.

Job Fairs and Industry Events

High-education establishments will stage regular job fairs to give students access to recruiters and employers. Studios build relationships with universities to gain direct access to fresh talent. Gaming expos, trade events, and other industry showcases may provide incredible opportunities. Studios and recruiters will set up stalls laced with swag to entice you at many major conferences and expos. These are often paid events, but they have freely accessible areas with developer booths and demos. These can be excellent places to chat with developers, get advice, and build connections.

Friends and Family

Knowing someone who works in the industry personally is advantageous. It's a privileged option that's not available to many. Let's be clear: a friend passing on your information to the hiring manager (and then exonerated from the process) is very different to the boss *hiring their mate* just because they can. Nepotism is favouring relatives or friends from a position of decision-making power. Studios often have financial incentives for successful candidate recommendations from employees (as the recommendation usually reduces risk). However, they still undergo the same process and scrutiny as those applying online or through external recruitment.

Quality Assurance (QA)

In the past, this vital role was once seen as an easy gateway job. Even now, you may read some articles online stating this fact. At one point, it may have been true. Many developers would start their careers in QA, and then eventually move to another role in development. Employers didn't require much experience or a degree; they just needed *a love for playing games* and general computer and literacy skills. Nowadays, this is not the case. The majority of internal QA teams are highly skilled and specialised developers and undergo a vigorous recruitment process. QA are the lifeblood of the industry and deserve respect.

I was very fortunate to start my career in QA. I learnt much about the industry's foundations and game production. I did not have even a percentage of the experience required now. Some applications are considered without industry experience, but you still will have to demonstrate your professional soft skills, and having a relative degree is advantageous.

Other Game Industry Roles

There are many roles outside of software development that are just as important in running a successful studio. These jobs include production, human resources/relations, finance, IT support, localisation, marketing, social media and community management, publishing, studio/office management, talent acquisition, and customer service. You may work in one of these fields and, mid-career, want to transition to software development. Luckily, you'll be surrounded by expert developers and technology to help you develop your skills.

Internal and External Recruiters

Internal recruiters are part of the studio team and will actively headhunt viable candidates for open roles. Never cold-call (solicitation with no prior contact) internal recruiters if their professional contact details are not public. It will demonstrate your level of creepiness rather than initiative.

Studios will also hire external recruitment agencies to widen the net. You can also sign up with an agency, too. They will attempt to find roles for you and apply on your behalf based on your specifications if they think you're suitable. The quality of recruiters can vary greatly. Be sure to verify their legitimacy. Some care about your career, helping you secure a role, building a good reputation, and promoting their business, while others are just after the commission, not reading your CV or prior work history, and spamming you into submission.

Etiquette

You can often judge a studio based on its recruitment process. (That's not to say a great recruiter and a poor studio are mutually exclusive.) But it can indicate how organised they are and how they value people. Note how they treat you throughout the process. Do they listen? Are they respectful of your time? Are they kind and inclusive? How transparent are they?

You cannot control or change how a company conducts itself. But you can control yourself. Before you apply for roles, review this checklist:

- Make sure your portfolio, CV, and cover letters are ready.
- Consider the method of communication and adhere to professional and personal boundaries.

- Update any online professional social profiles.
- Create a tracking sheet with all your applications. It's useful to keep track of what stage you are at, along with your contact details and outcomes. It may even help discover patterns, and you can note any feedback you receive to help update your CV and assets.
- Ask the recruiter what the process will look like and what to expect at each stage.
- Learn the names of those interviewing you and some professional information about them.
- Request detailed feedback after an interview if it's not provided automatically.
- Be excited to apply for a position at that studio, even if it's not your number one choice.
- Make bespoke applications, not copy and paste jobs.
- Figure out beforehand what you want to earn and what you want to achieve.
- Know your start dates and contracted notice periods.
- Don't be afraid to follow up or chase correspondence, but don't pester either.
- Treat everyone as you would want to be treated. If an organisation doesn't act that way during the process, that's your first 'red flag.'

Red Flags

'Red flags' are subtle (or not so subtle) indicators or warnings of potential issues in a person or organisation. They may not all be deal breakers, and, sometimes, you must consider what you can and can't tolerate based on situation and circumstances. Often, they are a clear indication that your values don't align or that the quality of the employer is lacking, and you can avoid wasting time and energy.

- There are too many lengthy interview stages across many months.
- Massive gaps between correspondence, 'ghosting,' or unresponsiveness.
- Generally poor or rude communication.
- An unnecessarily lengthy art test that feels like free work.
- The different people turning up than you were due to meet, without reasonable explanation.
- They are late starting an interview without reasonable explanation or acknowledgement.
- Offering deals they can't substantiate.
- They haven't looked at your portfolio or CV.

- The recruiter then didn't realise you used to work there.
- They ask generic questions—or haven't prepared any.
- Refusal to discuss compensation.
- Use non-inclusive language and make morally questionable comments.
- *"We are a family"* (Run for the hills!).

DON'T PANIC!

Excellent. All your hard work preparing and applying for a new job has paid off. You have landed yourself an interview. The date and time are sorted, and you have adequate preparation time.

British Army trainers established a saying in WWII known as the Seven Ps. *Proper Planning and Preparation Prevents Piss Poor Performance.* Planning ahead of time or a plan to fall back on will help your nerve and avoid a *piss-poor performance*.

Interviews can be a very intense experience for some, especially if it's your first time. I like to think interviewers are empathic to this, as they must have gone through a similar situation once in their lives. Many bad interviewers and their *techniques* have created this dark stigma around the process. Some play head games, ask *gotcha* questions, or don't act like human beings at all. The best interviews feel like a conversation and a natural discussion of character, competency, and cultural fit. In either scenario, being prepared will help you to feel comfortable.

The Pocket, Pocket Guide to Surviving Interviews

- DO YOUR RESEARCH! Most interviewers start with the standard, "What do you know about our studio?" So be ready for this. Don't lie, and try to make something up in the moment. You don't need to know their last fiscal reporting numbers; you need some general information about their past projects and company values. The question is a warm-up and designed to ascertain your legitimate interest. If they spent time learning about you, it's the least you can do.
- If you are interviewing remotely, be ready at your computer or phone fifteen minutes before the interview. Test that your microphone, camera, and headset are working.

- If it's on location, try to arrive early, too. You may have travelled far, so you might need a few minutes to freshen up, get a drink, stop sweating, and relieve yourself.
- During the interview, be polite and wait for people to finish speaking. Practise active listening and take your time responding. If they say something you want to comment on, write down a note so you can return to it later.
- If remote, have your CV, portfolio, and prepared questions on a secondary screen. On location, have a laptop or tablet (or printout) available.
- Remembering names in conversation will help make the experience more personal.
- During the interview, taking notes, details, and new questions is okay. However, they can't see you do this remotely, so try not to look like you are responding to emails and not paying attention. In both instances, don't let note-taking distract you from the conversation.
- When the interview is over, write down all the questions they asked you and your answers if you remember them, and put them in your tracker. You can review it later. If your question didn't clarify the information you sought, consider wording it differently next time.
- Remember, most people (on both sides) don't usually remember everything said, just how they felt, the energy of the room, and body language. Most interviewers have a list of words they want to hear and cross off.
- Stay hydrated. Have a drink before you start and some water at hand. Don't worry about having a drink between answering questions, as this gives you a natural pause to think and prevents you from drying up halfway through a sentence.
- Avoid too much caffeine immediately before an interview.
- Try having a healthy snack before an interview so you have some brain fuel in your system.
- If you feel nervous before an interview, try replacing nervous energy with kinetic energy. Dance or do light exercise.
- If you feel nervous before a call (or quietly on your phone before an in-person interview), watch a short video that makes you laugh or smile. Exposure to some endorphins, or dopamine, can take the edge off and put you in a positive mood.
- Avoid 'doom-scrolling' social media before the interview. You might see something that distracts you or puts you in a negative mood.

- Maintain good hygiene and dress appropriately for in-person interviews. If the interview is remote, ensure that the top half is presentable.
- Practice your interviews if you have time.
- Practice patience. I've seen candidates brimming with enthusiasm just waiting to interrupt someone speaking. Enthusiasm is great, but you need to keep your composure.
- Don't be afraid to pause after being asked a question and take a deep breath before answering. It's okay to think about your response.
- Don't over-prepare. Too many notes and windows open on the screen can become overwhelming.
- Before it all starts, take three deep, long breaths. And remember, don't panic.

Answering Questions

Answering questions in an interview can sometimes be intimidating, even scary. Some questions are purposefully written to trip you up or are just generic, poorly phrased questions from a book written forty years ago. Hopefully, you will be interviewed by modern people asking progressive questions designed to work as part of a conversation to help find out more about you.

(Good) Interviewers aren't looking to try and 'break' you. They are not forcing you to spill the secret launch codes. All they want to do is get an idea of how you communicate, your competency, and how well you would fit the studio culture and team. You must understand that the interview usually has a few critical things they need to hear you say and check off to affirm in their mind that you are a viable candidate for the role when they give feedback on the interview and when potentially making an offer.

This won't be an exhaustive list of questions and the correct responses. You must dig deep and remember that the best responses feel natural; an interviewer will detect rehearsed answers. Sticking to a script can land you in trouble when you suddenly have to go off it. We must try to understand what keywords the interviewer might need to hear with each question.

Try writing a response to the following questions using a few simple keywords and then answering them out loud without looking at your notes. Focus on keeping it concise and getting the main point across without adding filler or going off on a tangent. You want them to retain this in their minds afterwards—because they won't remember your exact words. Remember, many of the answers to their questions are in the job spec you already have.

A caveat on the questions below: I am not saying these are *good* interview questions—I hate most of them—but they are commonly used. Let's begin.

1. What do you know about the studio already?
2. *Why do you want this position?*
3. *What can you bring to this role?*
4. *Describe your work ethic.*
5. *What are you most proud of in your career so far?*
6. *Tell us about when you've had to manage multiple tasks or projects with complex requirements and competing priorities.*
7. *What motivates you?*
8. *Tell me about a time you failed.*
9. *Tell us about a time you've had to manage a difficult situation.*
10. *What are your greatest strengths?*
11. *What do you consider to be your weaknesses?*
12. *Tell me about a time you disagreed with a decision made at work and how you dealt with it.*
13. *What are you looking for salary-wise?*
14. *What is your current notice period?*

The Good, the Bad, and the Stupid Questions

If you're not getting helpful answers to the questions *you ask* in an interview, hopefully, this part of the chapter can help.

Interviews are generally not in people's top ten most enjoyable experiences. However, at the end of your interview, when asked, "Do you have any questions for us?" don't say no and run away—as tempting as that might be. Of course, if, during the interview, you decide that this job isn't for you, then you can decline politely. Professional interviewers will have time set aside for you to ask questions at the end, and this could be your only chance to ask important questions that make them feel like you are someone who already works there.

Firstly, we need to define what a "good," "bad," and a "stupid" question is. I know everyone says there is no such thing as a stupid question. But this is not true. That phrase typically applies to asking questions when you don't know anything about something. I think a stupid question is asking something already available to you, thus wasting everyone's time. Asking an employer what benefits they have if they have already listed them on the advert is not worthwhile. Of course, if you need clarity on some of them, that's fine to ask.

Questions that generally result in yes, no, or one-word answers are "bad." There are exceptions, but usually, you gain little to no additional insight—just confirmation. You want an interviewer to have to elaborate, and those short answer questions make it much easier for people to mask the truth or tell you what you want to hear.

You: "Is this a collaborative work environment?"

Them "- Yes."

Great, you have learnt nothing. You are not formatting the question, so it requires a detailed response. And that is what I would call a "good" question. Something that requires the recipient to think deeper and reveal more. Elucidate. Explain their words and bring value. Asking *if* the culture is collaborative is not as good as asking *how* they make the culture collaborative and *why* it's important. If they start stalling on this one, then maybe that tells you more than a blanket 'Yes,' as perhaps it's not a culture of collaboration, and they are trying to find a way of not saying that. With this mindset, you learn more by asking questions that don't suck.

Asking Questions That Don't Suck!

Let us break down a few questions I think are 'good' to ask. Don't ask any of these if they have already answered them in some form earlier in the interview.

What does success look like if I was working here?

You will hopefully hear how they value people, their work, their review and performance processes, and their promotion and bonus scheme. If they don't give you any details on this, they are either in a position in the studio that has no visibility of this, or the studio's process is terrible, which is a good answer … to why you should look elsewhere.

What advice would you give me if I were hired to help me succeed here?

Or, *"If I were to start today, how would you best use my skills in the project?"*

These are very confident-sounding questions—without sounding arrogant. You subtly encourage them to visualise you in the role as if you already work there. They are prompted to give you proper career advice and guidance as if they would as your manager. You will learn what sort of leader they are. They will appreciate your desire for self-directed improvement. You obtain an understanding of what the metrics are for measuring productivity. You want to know how to satisfy those metrics—and now they know that.

What were some of your team's most significant challenges this past year?

This question demonstrates that you are here for the good and hard times. They will see you are supportive and interested in helping them face challenges head-on. The answer to this question should teach you a lot about the stability of the studio, your future bosses, and potential teammates, whether it be a short or long answer. They may not always be able to answer this with anything specific due to contracts or data protection. Still, interviewers always answer questions somehow, so you will still learn something new.

What is the studio's culture like? In terms of hierarchy, management, social, and community,

Is there a strong sense of support, camaraderie, and so forth—how would they describe it? 'Family' is a huge red flag, often used to exploit your passion for free labour or to guilt you into complicity. When you have applied for thirty "families" in one week, the novelty wears off. A sense of community is great, but you don't want to join a cult.

How much autonomy comes with the role?

What this question really asks is, *Am I going to be micro-managed?* Am I expected to manage my time and be responsible for my workload? How much say do I have? Can I give feedback? What is the review process like? What happens if I screw up? Can I speak up without getting shut down?

If you could add or remove anything from my resume, portfolio, or even this interview today, what would they be?

There is no guarantee you will get the job or that you'll get feedback afterwards. This might be your only opportunity to gain valuable insight into what you could have done better. It will enable all parties to gain clarity and be open and honest. You might be able to put their concerns to rest then and there. We can address a misunderstanding or direct them to something they might have missed in your CV or portfolio, which satisfies the feedback.

Notice a theme with all these? None were like, *"What time do the free snacks arrive?"* or *"Do you like working here?"* They just drilled you for an hour. It's only fair that you get to do the same. No softballs, no easy answers. If you've walked away learning nothing new and only with information you could have found out with a quick Internet search, that is an unbalanced interview, and you need to start using that short window of time to ask better questions.

You will probably only have time for two or three questions at the end, but don't worry. If you run out of time, ask if it's okay to email a few more questions—a good interviewer should oblige.

ART AND DESIGN TESTS

Art tests (almost always unpaid) can sometimes be a necessary evil. In general, I am not a fan. However, when scoped well, with managed expectations and realistic time limits, they can be helpful when assessing the very best applicants as part of or in the final stages of the interview process—if they are, in fact, necessary. A candidate might hit all the boxes and demonstrate exceptional skills, but when given a reasonable brief, a time constraint, and limited resources (as they would on the job), they completely fall apart. Art tests should never be used as a blanket approach to recruitment.

The issue is that you never know what people are going through. It's okay if you have the available time or are between jobs. But if you work full-time and have responsibilities after work, that extra time must come from somewhere, potentially impacting your health, career, and relationships. I get that sometimes you have to dig deep with some extra effort to achieve changes in your life, but I think it's a lot to ask someone to do this.

I've only ever interacted with two art tests in my career—with me as the person being tested. The first one I received was for a big franchise. I was tasked with making assets for their game currently in production, and I flatly refused. The second test was a disaster. I couldn't achieve the quality I wanted while working full-time and at my current skill level. And therein lies my real *beef* with the whole concept. Art tests should be fair to the candidate and provide helpful new information for the interviewer. As a candidate, you must consider if you have time to do it without burning out. Does the test sound like free work or something that demonstrates my creative thinking and skills? As an interviewer, ask yourself, is this fair, achievable, and practical? Are we just doing this as a lottery and taking the responsibility away from ourselves in the decision-making process, or will we yield helpful data from this taxing initiative? Is the scope and duration of the brief reasonable? Does it account for work and life commitments? Is it realistic to ask someone working full-time if they even have time to do this?

A good art test needs to be abstract and a test of objective thinking, skills, and creativity—a simple proposal with various outcomes, not simply checking that they can recreate what you already do. It would be best to allow an applicant to show off some of their personality and ideas within the brief. The test parameters should demonstrate how well they deliver, elevate, and figure things out. The best art tests conclude with the candidate receiving professional, constructive feedback regardless of whether they secure the position or not. They deserve recognition and an opportunity to discuss things.

KNOW YOUR WORTH!

Knowing your worth is one of the most complex parts of your career. Appreciating and demonstrating our unique value can take some time and experience. Sadly, most jobs don't disclose salary. While a few provide salary ranges, many organisations prefer to remain competitive, avoid acknowledging pay inequities, or lack transparency. Even organisations with substantial income will often mask their financial situation and prefer to see you make the first move. It's bizarre.

During the interview, you may be asked the following question: *What salary are you looking for?* Some studios will already have a budgeted figure. Your objective is not to undersell yourself and end up with a **** deal while not overpricing yourself to the point where you are not hireable. You do not have to tell them what you were paid before.

As a working adult, you have responsibilities in life. You must pay rent and a mortgage, feed yourself, possibly smaller versions of yourself, and do things outside of work. So, when considering how much you should get compensated for dedicating your time and efforts to someone else, you must factor in a baseline of what you need to survive.

Following this, you also must research the average salaries for your position in your part of the world. Glassdoor or a simple Google search can help you with this, but you must keep the location and studio size in mind. Studios based in major cities are expensive to live in and usually have higher salaries. A smaller indie studio might not be able to offer you as big a salary as major corporations but may offer remote work or be located in cheaper places to live.

Along with your salary, remember that perks and benefits also form part of your compensation package. Annual leave, sick pay, pension, medical cover, paternity and maternity leave, bonus schemes, transport discounts, and merchandise can significantly change the perception of a wage. Also, consider the quality of life aspects like learning and development initiatives, flexible time, and covering relocation costs.

The last part to factor in is financial growth. You want to get a better deal than you had last time. If it's your first time, you want to get the best deal, but with fewer chips to bargain with—your goal is to cover the whole *food and water thing*. It would be best if you were realistic but safe. Generally, you want to ask for enough to be compensated correctly above market value and inflation, with enough to allow you to build a life and save comfortably. Don't ask for the moon; just enough to help get you there.

When entering into negotiations, consider your use of language and depersonalise the situation. You are not asking the interviewer but the company, so treat them separately. Make it about the business. Don't say, *"Would you?"* and instead say, *"Would Studio X?"*

Bring your value to the conversation; employers want to know what you can do for them, not what they can do for you. Don't say, *"I am looking for,"* but instead say, *"I'm currently interviewing for positions that pay X to Y."* *Looking* makes it sound aspirational, as if you are not worth it yet, whereas *currently* emphasises it as being the market's demands.

When making an offer, ask for more than what you want so that you are still happy when they return with a lower counteroffer. Psychologically, you want them to feel like they are getting a great deal while you achieve what you wanted. If they accept the original offer, that is great too, or they might say it's too low and bring it up to be in line with their other employees. Be confident and realistic, and know your numbers. Remember, this is your *starting* salary. Good studios conduct annual pay reviews, increase salaries with inflation, promotions, and award bonuses for project milestones.

ACCEPTANCE AND REJECTION

You've done it! You have passed their crude tests and whatever else they have thrown at you. They have agreed to your terms, and an offer has been made.

Ensure you read all the documentation. You can ask a family member or friend to help you if needed. Most contracts are relatively boilerplate (standard), so you shouldn't need to hire an employment lawyer to review them. Remember, you are still in the negotiation phase. If something reads as a potential concern or issue, politely raise it as a question with the hiring manager.

Your future employer may request referrals from past employers or higher education, so ensure you have provided the correct contact details. Remember to select solicited referrals from professionals who know your worth, support you, and remember you. I wouldn't stress this part too much; the new studio usually wants to confirm that your work history is accurate.

Visa applications might need to be arranged, and relocation challenges might need to be discussed. The studio should support you with everything you need once the process begins.

However, sometimes you don't receive an offer but get rejected. It happens. It's a highly competitive industry. It can be chaotic and unpredictable. Studios can close overnight, budgets get slashed, and projects get shelved just as fast. You might get to the end of a process and decide to go with someone else or feel they no longer need the role. It's essential to manage your expectations going into the process and have backup plans. Be ready to move on to the next application.

For your mental health and self-esteem, it's helpful to remember that if you are rejected or ghosted, it's not about you. *It's never about you.* We invest so much of ourselves, our time, into the process and put ourselves in a position to be vulnerable. It's a challenge not to get emotional or take it personally. Speculation isn't healthy or productive.

We may never know the whole story or what is happening behind the scenes. The studio is looking for a solution, but *they* haven't found it. Decisions are seldom made solely based on your performance. If you've put in your best effort and prepared to the fullest, there's nothing more you could have done. If you give anything your best shot, you'll never miss. Many rationales behind hiring decisions may never be made apparent to you. It can very often be an internal thing. We have to refocus rejection as an opportunity. It sucks for sure, but what can we learn from the process?

To better deal with rejection, be polite and graceful and ask for feedback if they don't send it with the rejection. Some AAA studios use automated systems for applications, and you can't directly communicate with them—which sucks—but you've got to appreciate that they receive hundreds of applications from hoax candidates and bots every day. Keep a cool head when corresponding, and take what you have learnt to the next one. This is just another step on your path. In the rare instance you get disrespectful or discourteous responses, well then … you dodged a bullet.

DAY ONE

Whether it is your first day at a new job or in the industry, it can be both exhilarating and nerve-wracking. Walking into a new studio, meeting new colleagues, and diving into unfamiliar tasks can bring excitement and apprehension. There are a few things that you can do to help prepare and make a positive first impression.

1. Before the big day, confirm your start time. Confirm your first call time if it's a remote job, but be set up and ready to go before then. A remote employer will send you information, hardware, passwords, and software before the start date.
2. Bring whatever ID or official documents you were asked to provide on the day.
3. Pay attention when being shown around the office.
4. If it's not your first job, don't discuss your past job with your new team like it was an ex you are still infatuated with. It can get really annoying. Equally, this isn't a race for everyone to get to know you—you don't need to deliver your whole CV to everyone you meet—it can come across as showing off.
5. In some studios, the CEO, studio director, or owners might come and introduce themselves on your first day. To make a good

impression, do yourself the service of learning who they are before they do this.

6. Remember, if anything goes wrong or you make a mistake, you always have the patented, get-out-of-jail-free card: *"Sorry, I am new. It's my first day."* However, that currency only lasts a month.

7. Don't hesitate to ask questions.

8. *Actually* read all the HR information you are provided.

9. Get involved promptly. Acquire invites to the meetings, sprint planning, and communication channels that are relevant to you.

10. Your line manager, IT, and HR should have scheduled meetings and a proper induction. If they haven't, politely request it. Cover topics such as expectations, best practices, goals, and responsibilities.

11. When you feel more settled in, you can request time with your direct peers to ask them questions and get to know them, perhaps over a coffee.

Any worthwhile studio will make every effort to make your first day and first week informative, welcoming, and supportive. Be practical with your time also. Be proactive in getting to know the project and the new team. Set up your workspace, familiarise yourself with the technology, and read the project documentation. Crazy thought: try playing the game.

Lastly, you might be sitting there thinking that you don't deserve this, that the people around you feel you are no good, or that your skills don't match what they are doing. This notion in your mind can be debilitating. *Imposter syndrome* is especially prevalent in those just starting. However, many have experienced it throughout their careers. I will ask you to consider the following truths if you ever experience these feelings.

1. No one expects you to know everything
2. You are still learning—we should all *still* be learning
3. The people around you probably feel the same way. They are just better at hiding it
4. Even if you have been doing the job for a while and still feel this way, it's okay. It's human

Acknowledging our weaknesses helps us identify areas for improvement. You can equate it to modesty. We often overestimate what is expected of us. Don't be afraid to ask questions and ask for help.

You got this.

Backup

10

INTRODUCTIONS

Until now, you've primarily heard my opinions, experiences, biases, and privileges from me. The following chapter introduces you to a community of professionals with insights into UX and UI game development. I asked each developer for advice on applying for jobs in this field, and what they consider the most crucial aspect of creating a great experience. The goal was to provide a broad range of exciting parallels and unique perspectives.

The thoughts expressed in the following interview excerpts are those of the individual giving them, not their organisation. I want to take this opportunity now to thank them again for their contributions.

Ian Plater

Sr Creative Director, UI/UX / PlayStation Studios: Creative

When we look to hire in our department, the main things we look for are: Presentation. The quality of your work and how you are able to talk about it. At its core, we are looking for a rationale behind the decisions you made during the design process.

Ideas. Anyone can follow the latest trend, but how are you breaking the rules and exploring new design ideas and spaces? We want to see a diverse range of ideas, styles, and solutions. Your failed ideas, or ones that didn't quite make the cut. We're also interested in your side hustles, and how this creativity manifests itself in other areas of your life.

Passion. Our team all love games UI/UX. We geek out about settings menus and outstanding design, so this isn't a stop-gap until we get the job we really want. We're aware that passion comes across in different ways. If you love your craft, this always comes through.

DOI: 10.1201/9781003367116-10

In games UI/UX, I believe the most interesting and challenging aspect is the crossover between entertainment and usability. If we consider entertainment and use the example of movie UI, its primary function is to sell the overall narrative and establish the world and characters. In addition, we have usability. If we use the example of a simple bank app, the primary purpose is to achieve your objective, such as checking your account balance, in an easy and intuitive way. Games UI/UX relies on a careful balancing of these two factors. Determining when to teach the player, when to be playful, and when to provoke an emotion are the decisions we make on a daily basis. By considering both these approaches, the game's intended experience is realised by the player.

Julie McConnell

UXUI Lead / Bungie

One of my favourite *UI/UX-isms* is "everyone is a user, but not everyone is THE user." It's important to be able to analyse how you, as a player, are both similar to and different from your target audience (for example, if you're reading this book, you likely care more about typeface choice than your intended audience does). When you're evaluating your own work and soliciting feedback from your peers, remember to filter things through that lens and hold both perspectives in your mind. What you (or your colleagues) like best might not actually be the best thing for your intended player or end user.

Stephan Dube

Principal UX/UI Designer and Founder of UI Peeps.com
https://linktr.ee/stephandube

It's important to remember that players come in various forms, and having empathy and understanding for their perspectives can be highly beneficial. Creating detailed personas is a key step in this direction. For instance, accessibility has gained significant traction in the gaming industry for valid reasons. Studios that invest in providing strong accessibility options not only contribute positively to the gaming community but also stand to gain returns on their investment by expanding their player base.

The concept of representation holds substantial importance in the industry today. Inclusivity and diversity play a pivotal role in helping players relate to the game and fostering greater appreciation among them.

François Savarimuthu

Lead UI & UX Artist / Designer
https://linktr.ee/francoissava

It comes down to the three Fs: form, fit, and function. The product must be desirable, fit for purpose, and function in the intended way it was designed to be. It's critical that all three work together to provide a good UX. Additionally, working towards better accessibility for equal access for your product must be set in stone from the get-go!

Cari Watterton

Senior Accessibility Designer / Rebellion
www.linkedin.com/in/cari-watterton

Educate yourself. There are so many amazing resources to learn from, particularly talks and panels at conferences such as the Games UX Summit, Game Developers Conference, and Game Accessibility Conference. Through these talks, you can learn from industry professionals; most are available to watch for free online.

Practice Your Craft. Having a great portfolio is where every job starts. Learn your tools, and use things like the UX Tools Design Challenges or the We Can Fix It In UI Design Test to practice your craft and add to your portfolio. Review your work, identify your weak points and where you need to improve and take that into your next project. I love to use game jams for an intense stint of creation that lets me work with my friends, try something different and learn new things.

Grow Your Network. Attending industry events is a great way to meet people, but I found the most useful interactions for me were through mentoring. Through schemes like *LimitBreak* and *BAFTA*, I got one-on-one feedback and advice from industry professionals matched to my goals. Mentoring has been and continues to be my number-one recommendation for anyone looking to get into any area of games.

Accessibility! UX and UI contain a keyword—user. A user can be anyone, and it absolutely shouldn't be limited to just "average" players because those just don't exist. Everyone is different and has different capabilities, and accessibility benefits everyone, from adjusting difficulty to turning on subtitles. How long a user needs to read a piece of text varies, or if they're even able to read that text at all. Or how a user interacts with an interface in a way that is comfortable for them. While there are so many conventions, standards, and guides for UI/UX design, never forget that the user is not static, and designing with accessibility and flexibility in mind only enables more people to play.

David Mariscal

Advanced UI/RPG programmer / Rocksteady Studios

I firmly believe that practice makes perfect, and the impact of presenting a wireframe, a working prototype, or sketches of UI examples can speak louder than any promising text-only CV!

With the abundance of free tools available nowadays, having tangible examples of your creative work becomes one of the best-selling points for securing a job interview. These examples don't necessarily need to be interactive demos. Demonstrating how you would design the layout for a specific screen in a game you like (or a game you'd like to create) could be the best way to showcase your workflow and skills in UI/UX design for games! As someone without formal UI/UX training, finding the right advice to give is genuinely challenging. I personally don't think there are better traits than others to have. It all boils down to the specific skill set a given company is looking for at a given time.

Rachel Brett

Junior Concept Artist and UX/UI Designer / Pie Trap Studios

Make networking your primary task—with kindness and authenticity! Breaking into any industry can be very challenging, even with good contacts. Still, it will be virtually impossible without them unless your portfolio is phenomenal (which it likely won't be if you haven't worked in the industry before). The thing about networking, though, is that you have to treat it like making friends (while maintaining professional boundaries), and not like finding stepping stones. Get to know them, ask questions you think they would be excited to answer, and be kind. Everyone has a radar for those connecting with genuine intent versus those trying to use others for personal gain. Authenticity is magnetic.

Be excellent to yourself, too. You will face a lot of obstacles, failures, and disappointments. It will sour your experience, and there will be a temptation to quit, blame yourself, or blame others. It's okay to feel down or doubt yourself, but don't let the setbacks control your actions. If you know deep in your gut that there is a true calling for this work, keep in touch with that feeling. Be patient, resilient, and self-compassionate. Tenacity and kindness put you where good luck finds you.

The best trait a designer can have is curiosity. Hold on to the student mindset; be humble and progressive in your thinking. Learn from your seniors and educate yourself every day. Ask, "How can I do better and be better?" There is no ceiling on growth.

Jonathan Tyler

UI/UX Designer / Wizards of the Coast/Hasbro

To excel in gaming UI/UX, it's not just about design skills. Diving into game engines like Unity or Unreal is important to learn how to implement your work effectively. Understand the entire game development process at a high-enough level to make discussions; it's key to staying competitive. Producers, engineers, and designers appreciate those who grasp the bigger picture, making it easier to discuss what is needed for the game and success in your position.

Rami Majid

Graphic/UI Designer / HypGames
www.linkedin.com/in/rami-majid

Hiring managers want to see what you are capable of and your passion for the work and process. I found joining modding groups and/or fan-made projects fun, educational, and rewarding. You will learn much from your mistakes and understand what to expect from a real-world scenario. It gives you a great portfolio piece to showcase during interviews and provides you with many things to speak about, such as the process, problems encountered, and solutions.

Try to look at designs from a global viewpoint. Anyone anywhere should be able to pick up and digest information and interact intuitively. I do believe that should you succeed in creating a simple, effective, and accessible UI/UX, it will go unnoticed because it feels so natural to interact with.

Gavin Marshall

UI Technical Designer & UI Artist / EA DICE
www.gavmakesgames.com

It all begins with creating. Consistently making new things, whether big or small, will only help you and your portfolio grow. It's important to showcase your niche in your CV and portfolio clearly. The more "generalist" you appear, the harder it becomes to convey your passion for the UI/UX crafts.

Working outside the games industry in a UI/UX role is still a great way to gain experience and, eventually, land a job in games. As long as you market yourself as someone who is interested in working in games, and your portfolio reflects that, you can go a long way.

Lastly, use social media to your advantage. Showcase your abilities, speak about your interests, and build a network on sites like LinkedIn. Engage with recruiters about currently open roles once you've applied and let them know you're interested. So long as you remain humble, social media can open many doors for you.

It may seem obvious, but don't forget what the UI/UX acronyms actually stand for! A functional menu with a great, accessible UX design will outperform any experimental UI every day of the week. Of course, there's a balance to be struck here, but when you're designing, it's always important to consider the logistics of your implementation. As you create something, think about how a player might experience it, and look for pain points, removing as many as you can without over-designing.

Casia Dominguez

Lead User Interface Designer
www.cassiainteractive.com

One crucial piece of advice is to prioritise simplicity and clarity in your UI design. Players should intuitively understand how to navigate menus, access essential information, and perform in-game actions without unnecessary confusion or frustration. Streamlining the UI not only enhances the overall gaming experience but also ensures that players can fully immerse themselves in the game world. Establishing a cohesive visual and interactive style helps players feel more comfortable and confident using the interface. This consistency can extend to fonts, colour schemes, button layouts, and iconography. When players can rely on these familiar elements, they can focus on the gameplay itself rather than struggling to adapt to a constantly changing interface.

Braden League

UI Technical Artist / 343 Industries

To get a job in games I believe the most important thing is to demonstrate your ability to finish a project, and I would almost weigh this higher than an individual's quality of work. I believe this is true for the game UIUX as well. Mockups are great, but I get more excited by actually playing a finished game or completed prototype. I would recommend taking part in game jams or completing a project you have in a course. Finishing projects is one of the hardest things you can do, and I personally have a plethora of unfinished personal projects, but these days, I value finishing something more than making it good. I firmly believe that you learn so much more by completing a project than by making something actually good.

Holly Hilson

Associate Experience Designer / Codemasters—EA Sports

When I graduated from university, I struggled to get a role in the industry. In fact, it took over 3 years before I got my first role. The key aspect that helped me was to open up my search. Jobs outside of games helped me get a step closer to getting my first games industry role. You will still learn key design principles for mobile apps and websites that will be transferable.

There are game-adjacent/separate industries, for example, E-Learning and Serious Games in which companies use game engines and art software, where you can learn and practise key skills, from conception to implementing interfaces. This can also help you create case studies and portfolio pieces that can become great discussion points during your application process.

Don't stop learning after graduation. There are some fantastic courses on websites such as Coursera and Udemy that can help you push your work to the next level. These can help bridge any gaps of knowledge you may have, depending on what course you have taken to get to this point.

I've also found networking to be important. It's been key for my further learning and has also helped me with receiving feedback from companies. Coming out of a games art degree as the only student wanting to niche into UI art, it was hard to find resources when you aren't surrounded by like-minded people. It's easy to lose the drive to get your first industry role. I thoroughly recommend the We Can Fix It With UI Discord channel, where everyone was so welcoming and knowledgeable.

Max Vizard

UI/UX Designer / Playground Games

As someone who took a longer route into the industry, I thought I would be an anomaly. But a surprising number of UI people often come from design / marketing backgrounds. Don't be afraid to make the leap. There are plenty of transferable skills. However, what is vital is to develop an appropriate portfolio. My method was to find some concept art on Artstation that I found inspiring and then develop a HUD overlay for that scene. It is also helpful to pander to your prospective employers, for example, If you wanted to work at Naughty Dog, it wouldn't make sense for you to create a super fleshed-out sci-fi UI. As with all good designs, design with intent, especially when building your portfolio.

Georgeth Lyver

UX Designer / Epic Games
www.georgethlyver.com

I suggest getting real experience creating a game, no matter how small that game may be. When I first started to learn about UX design for games, I did a lot of case studies on my own. Doing this got me into the habit of following one rigid design process, which is vastly different from what your day-to-day role will be like as a UI/UX designer. When I participated in a game jam, I saw the potential to utilise various different skills and tweak my design process to account for the specific needs of the game and the time constraints we were faced with. This experience helped me break away from the one design process and taught me how important collaborating with others is to your design, which is what helped me prepare the best for working in the industry. So, participate in game jams, grab some friends with a wacky game idea, and make something cool together! Just don't forget to document it in your portfolio later.

The most crucial thing to remember when trying to craft a great UX is that crafting the user's experience is not limited to one person who holds the title of "UX designer." It is the culmination of many people's hard work, and ensuring that there is a high level of communication among all disciplines every step of the way will help reach that desired final product. UX requires a lot of collaboration, even when you're just conceptualising what that experience could be for users. Keep an open dialogue, listen to folks with varying specialities, and watch how everyone's efforts and voices build a great UX.

Nida Ahmad

Game UX Designer
www.nidaahmad.me

Have a portfolio that shows your design process and UX thinking. This typically includes case studies; for me, my first portfolio was a UX breakdown of popular titles as my interests are within UX strategy, the UX/game design crossover, and psychology. Lean into your specific interests if you don't know—experiment!

Search for roles that reflect your values and goals for the type of UX or UI professional you want to be. This helps keep you grounded, and finding a company that aligns with you in that respect will help minimise the chances of burnout or dissatisfaction.

Foster relationships with others. Networking will help you find roles but also build connections that will support you in navigating and growing within this volatile industry. Check out communities such as We Can Fix It In UI or IGDA Games Research & UX SIG.

Keep on learning! You want to keep building your expertise that will make you a valuable hire. Keep up-to-date with the latest research and UX and UI trends by playing games and checking out Edd Coates' Game UI database. There are amazing books out there such as *Games User Research* (Drachen, Nacke and Mirza-Babaei), *Game Usability* (Isbister and Hodent), and *How To Be A Games User Researcher* (Bromley).

Prioritise your well-being above all. As a "passion"-oriented industry, it's easy to get lost in the rat race and compare yourself to others. Remember that comparison is the thief of joy, and you will thank yourself in the long run for taking care of your health.

Kylan Coats

Founder/Creative Director / Crispy Creative
www.kylancoats.com

Have a portfolio and be able to speak to it. If you don't have professional experience, you can still fill out a portfolio. Select a UI screen in a game you enjoy (e.g. the Inventory Screen in Fallout or the HUD in Call of Duty) and redesign it. Not just the art style but also the UI design and UX flow. Talk about why you made the changes you did and how the redesigned screen still works within the game. Include the redesign as a personal project in your portfolio. This not only shows that you've been through the UI/UX process but also reveals how you think and approach interfaces in games.

Game dev is a marathon, not a sprint. To stay in it for the long term, you've got to learn how to learn. Don't ever get tied too closely to one set of tools. Be sure you're at least a little familiar with whatever's on the horizon.

Sarah Robinson

Associate Art Director / Behaviour Interactive

In two decades of experience working with UI and UX, one thing stands out: rather than extensive schooling or work experience, prospective UI/UX designers are weighed primarily on the quality of their portfolios. Entry-level portfolios don't need to have a lot of examples. Two to three solid examples of your best UI/UX designs, wireframes, or flow documents can go a long way to showcasing what you can do. Make sure there is a broad range of art and game styles represented in your work.

There's a saying amongst industry veterans, "The best UI is an invisible UI." This doesn't mean literally not visible, but rather something effortless that players intuit how to use without you having to explain it. A good starting point is establishing a clear visual hierarchy. Break your UI into levels of what you want players to see or do first, second, etc. This will alleviate the cognitive load for your players and make it easier to play your game. And because you're already thinking about how players will experience your UI, piece by piece, you have a framework for how to approach all the other aspects of UI/UX design!

Edd Coates

Creator of the Game UI Database and PadCrafter

The most common mistake I see in portfolios is a lack of focus in the field people are aiming for. I've seen many UI/UX portfolios with 3D art, code, photography, etc. Some don't even have any game UI in them! While employers need to see that you're highly skilled, they also need to know that you're passionate about the field you're applying for and not just looking for *any* job in the games industry. Avoid being a jack-of-all-trades, and try to position yourself as a specialist instead. Unsure about focusing on UI or UX right now? That's fine! Create separate portfolios for each of your fields of interest. Not only does this allow you to apply for multiple types of jobs, but it's also useful for seeing which of your portfolios/skills gives you the most positive response and the best chance of finding employment. Just be aware that maintaining multiple websites (and skillsets!) can be very time-consuming, so it's better to decide on your focus sooner rather than later.

Although we as an industry have a habit of separating UI from UX, the truth is that UX and UI are intrinsically linked. Without an intuitive UX, the interface is worthless; therefore, it is absolutely critical for us to focus on usability before adding any additional flourishes.

Mary Yovina (They/Them)

UI/UX Lead / Insomniac
www.maryyovina.com

Understand the expectations of the position and get help assessing what it will take for you to meet those expectations. Seek out opportunities to have your portfolio reviewed, ask your peers for feedback, and look at the portfolios of people already doing the job you want. It's important to have your work reviewed because, ultimately, I think the most valuable advice is any that is specific to your own work.

Also, keep in mind that UI and UX positions aren't uniform in responsibilities across studios. You may be a perfect fit for a UI artist role at one studio but unqualified (and unhappy) to do a job with the same title at another studio that expects a combination of UI art and UX design skills.

UI/UX exists at the intersection of several disciplines, and we need to balance many wants and needs across departments as we design solutions. In order to do our best work, it's important to understand the game pillars, the narrative and art aspirations, and the feature designs—and it's important to understand the details of "why."

If we understand what the intended player impact is and what is important, then we can better understand how to approach the problem of designing the UI. With that knowledge, we can craft meaningfully appropriate solutions that reflect the identity of the game, with player experience in mind. By examining what we're doing and why, we are more likely to notice if something about the design is in conflict with any of our goals.

Kemal Akay

Lead Technical UI Designer / EA DICE
www.kemalakay.com

Entering the game industry in a UI or UX position can be both exciting and challenging. Some candidates think that having a background in frontend web or app design and development can be helpful. Although that's true, it's important to acknowledge that games have their own design language and can use custom tools. Therefore, showing a genuine passion for gaming and game UX design is always helpful. For instance, analysing your favourite game's HUD and using UX terminology to explain it in an interview can go a long way. Also, take your time to understand what you truly enjoy: What part of UI or UX makes you excited the most: design, art, or implementation? They all require problem-solving but understand which one allows you to get out of bed more quickly in the morning. Find your *Ikigai*.

Fundamentally, within the realm of UI/UX, our primary objective is to effectively convey gameplay information to players in the most comprehensible manner possible. There are no universal solutions for achieving this; every product requires a different approach based on their user stories. However, there are frameworks for identifying and addressing players' pain points. For example, one can conduct analyses of other games, study usability and engage-ability concepts from Celia Hodent, and get familiar with terminologies such as cognitive workload, game flow, signifiers, and feedback. Adopting this UX-oriented mindset and applying it can ensure that games provide functional and intuitive experiences tailored to the specific needs and preferences of the target audience.

Leah Chalkey

Senior UI/UX Designer / Rebellion
www.leah.chalkey.net

It's important to build a portfolio that showcases your skills. Your portfolio is the main thing an interviewer will look at when reviewing you for a UI or UX position. Make sure you put forward your best work. It's about quality, not quantity. How you present your work is as much of an indicator of your skills and attention to detail as the work itself. So take the time to consider the layout, formatting, and flow of the work in your portfolio.

At the start of your career, you might not initially have much to include in your portfolio, but there are lots of game UI design briefs available online that you can use to challenge yourself and create some work to present in your portfolio. Spending some time doing some self-motivated work like this can be something that really helps you stand out.

Ultimately, the foundations of building a good user UX lie in your initial research. It's really important to get hands-on and play games, especially with a critical eye. This will help you understand things from the user's perspective.

Usually, whenever I start working on a new project, I'll spend some time playing other similar titles. I create a competitor analysis document in which

I'll take some screengrabs or video footage and note the pros and cons of the features within each game. This helps me recognise similar trends, as well as what does or doesn't work and why.

While designing a game's UI, it's also really important to keep reviewing what you're doing. The same critical eye that was used to gather initial research should be employed in your own work. Join playtests, listen to any feedback you receive, and always try to understand why it's been given and how it will help the end user.

Jordan DeVries

UI/UX Lead (Jedi Team) / Respawn Entertainment
www.jordandevries.com

UI/UX is still an underserved niche in the game industry! In games, aspects like interactivity, immersion, and performance are far and way ahead of the broader tech industry, but the tech industry has significantly more mature theories and processes. Understanding this tension is key—if you're coming from tech, you have a lot to offer but a lot to learn.

Another common mistake I see is that when we build digital products, we put our thesis statements upfront (our hooks, our TL;DRs, etc) and provide skimmable, scannable ways to navigate; your resume and portfolio should be no different! Before you'll convince anyone in the hiring process to read through your pipeline, wireframes, etc, they often need to see a compelling enough finished product upfront to draw them in.

Generally, the broader UI/UX industry is singularly obsessed with removing friction. Most apps and websites are designed to funnel you, as quickly as possible, into a desired action (and usually it's to buy something). Game UI/UX is the complete opposite. Digging yourself out of a hole, overcoming a challenge, and feeling accomplished is the entire point.

A game with no friction is effectively a screensaver.

Chris Johnson

Lead UI Artist / Infinity Ward
www.kris-j.com

Showcasing your skills is key, so why not try game jams, redesigning existing UI in games, or doing online courses to level up your game? Don't forget to flaunt your skills! If you're the artsy type, get creative with eye-catching icons, smooth HUD animations, and screen mockups. If you're more tech-savvy, dive into Figma, Unreal, Unity, shaders, and scripting for some hands-on action.

Always let your intentions shine through and share the story behind your decisions. Seasoned developers have a keen eye, but taking them through your process step by step adds that special touch of passion that sets you apart. It makes all the difference!

You know the saying, "A great UI is invisible." It's so true. You've probably experienced games with slick UIs, and some not-so-great ones that make you scratch your head. It's a tough challenge for any studio, especially when games have intricate systems that could overwhelm players.

That's where the magic of a UX designer comes in—transforming complexity into something easily understandable. One thing you'll come to learn is that you can tweak the original feature design whilst keeping the essence intact. Don't be scared of this! What matters most is that players have fun. With insights from User Research and Playtests, even the most intimidating features can become player favourites!

As developers, we walk a tightrope. We've got this specific experience in mind for players, but we've got to be careful not to stumble. At the end of the day, it's all about the players, ensuring they're having a blast. Get that right, and they'll keep coming back for more, and that's when the real magic happens!

Between U and I

11

WHY UX/UI IS IMPORTANT

Thank you for reading this guide; I had no idea how best to end it. If it wasn't apparent by now, the astronaut was an allegory for the user, and the convoluted life support console represented the worst UX and UI imaginable.

So now what? I hope this is just the beginning, and you leave with a desire to learn more, try new things, or approach challenges with a different perspective. Maybe you'll stop asking people to *"make it pretty."* I'm kidding. Perhaps it was the jolt of energy you needed when things were low. If it made you laugh once, I'll be happy.

This book was written to be a helpful little mentor in your back pocket. But what does it mean to be a mentor? A mentor is not someone who teaches you stuff you can find out on your own. Anyone can impart information to another. A mentor provides guidance and support. To develop knowledge and values from another's experience.

If you are unsure what to do next after reading this, pass this book on to someone else, be a mentor yourself, and pay it forward.

I love what I do. I'm very fortunate that I make games for a living, and with each passing year, I still find UX and UI fascinating. I hate all the discourse and gatekeeping online about the two. The tools don't matter, only the craft. They are both equally intertwined. UX forms a unique and beautiful tag team with UI, the practical cousin that melds aesthetic form with function. What's not to love? Sure, it can be challenging at times. Anything worth doing will be. Ideas will fail, and scenarios will leave you wondering if it's worth it. There are hills you will die on and battles you will lose. So why do we do it?

In the past, not many people chose this path. Commonly, graphic designers would get into games, and UI was the best fit. Now, people are *actually choosing* this path, and that's really exciting. There are a lot of UX principles to learn. It's a lot to get your head around. I struggle to remember everything myself, yet I decided to write about it. I wouldn't expect you or anyone to learn all that by heart. But generally, you don't need to. The majority of it ends up feeling like common sense, and that's comforting. This extends into UI as well. Sometimes, you're making something, and you will find harmony in alignments that sit 'right' with a few unconventional nudges. A particular colour pops more. Two fonts that you wouldn't dream of putting together click. It's a feeling I can't describe.

If you apply for a job in UI, UX, or any discombobulation of the two, remember that the focus will be on how you present yourself. First impressions of someone whose job is creating *first impressions* are paramount. When hiring, we look at portfolios first, and raise eyebrows at a CV without any discernible flair or effort put into the content and presentation. There is a lot of noise in this space, so when something shines, it truly shines. We all gaze up in unison and say, *"damn, that is a lovely UI"* (I'm sure my colleagues and peers will relate to this).

Whether you've just secured your first job in the industry (congrats!) or moved to a new studio (congrats again!), understanding how a studio functions will always be an adjustment, especially regarding how it recognises UI and UX. Studios really are not all the same. I've worked in places with barely a glimmer of UX culture, and others structured like a well-organised symphony, where every element harmonises seamlessly, like instruments following a meticulously composed score. If I can offer advice, put one foot in carefully and get an idea of the current. It can be easy to deter people if some of these concepts are unfamiliar or don't align with their biases. You have to treat it like UX and adapt. Introduce changes and new ideas gradually.

The most valuable skill you can learn isn't the latest trending software or fancy new methods. It's communication. *Communication is interaction.* No matter the industry, lousy communication leads to bad results. It's not about who can talk the most, speak the loudest, answer the quickest, or dominate a meeting or email chain. How you communicate reflects you as a developer.

Being successful in UX/UI is about opening people's minds, and the best way to do that isn't to argue but to actively listen. Good communication is not only being clear and concise in verbal or written interactions—it's about non-verbal cues, too. It's ensuring your message is understood *and* everyone's input is respected. Because when people feel understood, they become less defensive and more reflective. They develop less extreme nuanced views. And, if they have any shred of empathy, they will appreciate that you listened and will attempt to listen to you. Listening to respond is not listening to understand. To understand is to be understood. If you only take away one thing from this guide, I hope it's the knowledge that harnessing and utilising this skill will trickle down into everything else you do. UX is a two-way street.

So why is UI/UX important in games?

If we've learnt anything, it's about the player. The ideal scenario is that anyone, no matter who they are, their struggles, or preferences, can pick up a controller and play the game like we weren't even here. We mutually want great experiences that delight and inspire. No one rushes to the store to buy the latest game for its UI and UX (and those that do probably work in the discipline). At best, we hope they walk away from the experience noticing nothing at all, and if they praise the visuals and functionality, that's a pleasant surprise. And we're okay with that.

Great UI/UX directly impacts the overall player experience, making the complex intuitive, enjoyable, and accessible, and the simple becomes a well-presented marvel.

BE KIND

I've been working on this book for a while now. The editing process has been enlightening. When I started the book, I was not in a happy place. We were leaving the tail end of the COVID-19 pandemic. Many had lost loved ones, shared dark times (at a distance), and felt the world change. For many of us, it was games that kept us together.

We saw a big boom in new audiences adopting games as a social activity, and others tried new games they wouldn't usually play. *Some even cleared a little of their Steam library backlog!* The games industry adapted. Studios were hiring more developers and still releasing games with all this going on.

Throughout the writing, I felt anger and negativity. I was upset by people in the past, toxic workplaces, and my mistakes. I was *burnt out.* In the seemingly typical fashion of *life*, many events followed suit. My dad was diagnosed with cancer, and I worked in new studios, moved cities, navigated redundancies, and learnt new skills I never thought I could do. My whole lifestyle changed.

When I began reading back, watching my words and attitudes change, I observed these stages as if they were rings inside a tree. I saw things shifting. I felt myself growing again, regaining confidence in what I could do, and becoming more accepting of things I couldn't change and how I handled them. I was becoming happier and kinder to myself.

Reflecting upon this, I learnt three key lessons:

- Kill negativity
- Escape your comfort zone
- Be kind

The games industry can be stressful, which is stupid, considering we make things that are supposed to be fun and bring people together. Negative traits are present in everyone, and they must be eradicated. Being judgemental and doubting yourself means focusing on the negative. Worrying, moaning, gossiping, complaining, and assuming the worst all the time means you become a source of negativity and set yourself up to be unhappy. You will attract negative people and continue to grow more and more hostile. If you always think things will not improve, they won't, and that's all you will focus on. You will end up trying to control everything in your work and life. It's not possible, and you have to kill it. Focus on what you are responsible for and take responsibility. You have to *kill* the negativity.

There are a few things you can do to help achieve this assassination. It begins with prioritising your work-life balance. Make more time for friends and family, exercise, and practice healthy mindfulness. You can even seek counselling or get a dog. (Dogs are probably cheaper.)

There are other forms of negativity. *Perfectionism* doesn't sound negative, but it can be, so you should kill it. Perfect is the enemy of good. We all want high-quality work, but it's about progress, not perfection. Leonardo Da Vinci is attributed to saying, "Art is never finished, only abandoned.' You are only as good as your time, resources, available skills, and budget allow. If you're always chasing perfection, you will never obtain it. The only person you are competing with is yourself.

To avoid the pit of perfectionism, you must accept that it's okay to fail. Just do it quickly. *Failing fast* refers to acknowledging when a particular approach is not working *quickly*. Minimise the time and resources invested in an unsuccessful path and rapidly shift towards something more promising. It's a counter to the *sunk cost fallacy*.

Failing fast leads to *"Getting to right."* The indescribable and poorly worded feeling when something starts to work and is suitable for the goal. The subtle art of recognising when something is good enough or could be better. "Right" doesn't mean 'perfect.' It needs to achieve the *right* goal. As soon as you can shift your mindset to the idea that progress and completing something is more important than perfection, you will start experiencing better results. Some of the best game features were happy accidents or entertaining bugs. Conversely, other features that are painstakingly worked on end up terrible. Constant iteration can become annoying. It's crucial not to overdo it.

When I started writing, I felt truly out of my depth. I thought, "What if people hate it?" and "What if it's not good enough?" I was speculating and growing anxious. I was leaving my comfort zone and letting negativity flow in.

The comfort zone is a psychological state where everything feels familiar; you're more at ease and in control. Activities and behaviours fit a routine that minimises stress, anxiety, and risk. Imposter syndrome presents itself when people are out of their comfort zone. To grow, you need to be a little bit uncomfortable. We become more sociable when we enter more social situations. We build muscles by increasing the weight. You may have heard the expression, "always play to your strengths" and thought, "Why not continue to do what I am good at? *I like my comfort zone.*"

The biggest enemy of contentment is *want*. Your comfort zone is not where you will become better. Always embracing our strengths means we never overcome our natural weaknesses. If you set your limits, you will never surpass them. We need freedom to fail, experiment, and tinker. Things we consider not to be strengths right now will eventually become them. However, goals must be achievable. Overwhelming yourself is not going to help your self-esteem and anxiety. (Try practising the 80:20 rule, where 80% of your work is stuff you are familiar with and 20% new things. Document your growth as you go. Take a screenshot or a video every day, and look back at the end and *see* what you learnt and how you grew.)

It's not about how much time and energy you use but how you use it. I measure success on the level of proficiency you demonstrate and if you deliver.

- Do I have good rapport and relationships?
- Am I being supportive and working in harmony with people?
- Am I innovating or coasting?
- Am I advocating for myself and others?

Be honest with yourself. Review your skills, output, and ideas and improve upon them. Stop focusing on getting promoted. Concentrate on what you are doing and enjoy what you do. Your worth is the value you bring, not how it's labelled. That's how it will be recognised.

The only thing you can truly control is yourself and your actions. Remember that other people's opinions or past failures don't define you. See them as opportunities to learn and grow, as they offer valuable lessons. Try every day to be better than the last and learn from your mistakes. Stay clear of the people who stomp down on others to feel 'taller' or try to pull you down to their 'level' only to prove that they are *beneath* you. Treat others how you want to be treated. Be the change you want to see. Make clear decisions about what you want and pursue your passions wholeheartedly. Stop procrastinating on important goals and delaying things that can be done today. Be open to learning rather than insisting on being right. Ask for help and be open to knowledge. Accept existing conditions or take responsibility for changing them. Doing the right thing is never the wrong thing. Face your problems directly and take decisive action instead of making excuses. Embrace the moment rather than becoming consumed by the past. Be honest with yourself and make happiness a choice. Wear sunscreen.

Life and career often involve unexpected and fortunate discoveries. Don't be discouraged by minor setbacks, and never underestimate the potential of small opportunities. Sometimes, the small twists of fate lead us to our most outstanding achievements.

And, most importantly, even when others are not, always be kind.

Useful Links

(not in order of usefulness)
ablegamers.org
specialeffect.org.uk
gameuidatabase.com
uipeeps.com
WE CAN FIX IT IN UI (@WeCanFixItInUI)
limitbreak.co.uk
interfaceingame.com
careerfoundry.com
interaction-design.org
hudsandguis.com
flaticon.com
typesetinthefuture.com
fontjoy.com
intogames.org
history.user-interface.io
lawsofux.com
gameindustrycareerguide.com

Further Reading

The Design of Everyday Things – *Donald Norman*

Emotional Design: Why We Love (Or Hate) Everyday Things – *Donald Norman*

The Gamer's Brain: How Neuroscience & UX Can Impact Video Game Design – *Celia Hodent*

What UX is Really About: Introducing a Mindset for Great Experiences – *Celia Hodent*

Blood, Sweat, and Pixels – *Jason Schreier*

Press Reset – *Jason Schreier*

Designing Interfaces – *Jenifer Tidwell, Charles Brewer, Aynne Valencia*

Don't Make Me Think, Revisited: A Common Sense Approach to Web (and Mobile) Usability – *Steve Krug*

A Theory of Fun for Game Design – *Raph Koster*

Games User Research – *Anders Drachen*

Gamify: How Gamification Motivates People to Do Extraordinary Things – *Brian Burke*

Universal Principles of Design – *William Lidwell*

Thinking with Type – *Ellen Lupton*

Printed in the United States
by Baker & Taylor Publisher Services